EXITS

E. P. Dutton ▲ New York

EXITS

Stories of Dying
Moments &
Parting
Words

Scott Slater
&
Alec Solomita

For information contact:
E. P. Dutton, 2 Park Avenue, New York, N.Y. 10016

Library of Congress Cataloging in Publication Data
Slater, Scott.
Exits: stories of dying moments & parting words.
Bibliography: p.
1. Last words. I. Solomita, Alec, joint author. II. Title.
PN6328.L3S6   1979   080   79-11696
ISBN: 0-525-93070-1

Published simultaneously in Canada by
Clarke, Irwin & Company Limited, Toronto and Vancouver

Designed by The Etheredges

10 9 8 7 6 5 4 3 2 1
First Edition

This book is lovingly dedicated
to our parents,
Nadia Koulischer Solomita, Vincent John Solomita,
Gwenyth MacEllven Slater and Philip Elliot Slater.

CONTENTS

ACKNOWLEDGMENTS **xi**

INTRODUCTION **xiii**

Tallulah Bankhead **2**

Henry David Thoreau **2**

Dominique Bouhours **3**

Henry Labouchere **3**

Sir Walter Raleigh **4**

Elizabeth Barrett Browning **4**

Ludwig van Beethoven **5**

Gustav Mahler **5**

Huddie Ledbetter
(Leadbelly) **5**

Ethel Barrymore **6**

Hart Crane **7**

Pablo Picasso **8**

Abram Hewitt **8**

Dr. Joseph Henry Green **8**

Nero **9**

Kusakábé **10**

Charles Darwin **11**

John Eliot **11**

John Morehead **11**

Dylan Thomas **12**

Turlough Carolan **13**

Sarah Bernhardt **16**

Paul Muni **16**

Georgiana Drew Barrymore **17**

Wolfgang Amadeus Mozart **18**

Frédéric Chopin	**18**
Napoleon Bonaparte	**19**
Sam Houston	**20**
Otto von Bismarck	**20**
William Pitt	**21**
John André	**21**
George Washington	**23**
Johann Wolfgang von Goethe	**23**
Victor Hugo	**24**
Augustus Bozzi Granville	**24**
Dr. Alexander Adam	**25**
Heinrich Heine	**25**
Herman Mankiewicz	**26**
Florenz Ziegfeld	**27**
Jack Rybakoff	**30**
Frank Kierdorf	**30**
Arthur Flegenheimer (Dutch Schultz)	**30**
Damon Runyon	**31**
Jimmy Walker	**32**
Charles Abbott	**33**
William Henry Harrison	**33**
John Quincy Adams	**33**
Lytton Strachey	**34**
Brian Piccolo	**34**
George Combe	**35**
Élie Metchnikoff	**35**
Dr. George Miller Beard	**36**
William Hunter	**37**
John Keats	**37**
Charlotte Brontë	**39**
Virginia Woolf	**40**
Barnett (Barney) Barnato	**40**
Cecil Rhodes	**41**
Robert S. Brookings	**41**
John Jacob Astor	**41**
Auguste Rodin	**44**
Vincent van Gogh	**45**
Jean Corot	**45**
Thomas Edison	**45**
Stephen Crane	**46**
William Allingham	**46**
Aldous Huxley	**46**
William Morris	**47**
George Bernard Shaw	**47**
Luigi Pirandello	**48**
Alexander Pope	**48**
Socrates	**49**
Phocion	**49**
Jacques Danton	**50**
Marie Antoinette	**51**
Madame du Barry	**52**
Joseph Addison	**53**
Giacomo Casanova	**54**
John Wesley	**54**
Aaron Burr	**55**
Solomon Foot	**55**
Thomas Paine	**55**
Fyodor Dostoevsky	**56**
Grigori Rasputin	**57**
Agrippina	**60**
Henry IV	**62**
Martin Luther King, Jr.	**62**

Frederick Douglass 63
Robert Louis Stevenson 63
Elinor Wylie 64
Oscar Odd McIntyre 64
Charles Parnell 65
William Wycherley 65
Oliver Goldsmith 66
Julius Beerbohm 67
William Gilbert 67
Oscar Wilde 68
Alfred Jarry 70
Ernest Dowson 71
Edgar Allan Poe 72
Charlotte Mew 74
Vachel Lindsay 74
Alice Meynell 76
Gerard Manley Hopkins 76

Charles de Ligne 78
Maria Theresa 78
Benjamin Franklin 79
Thomas Jefferson and John
    Adams 79
Daniel Webster 80
Henry Adams 81
Thomas Hobbes 82
Woodrow Wilson 82
Edith Piaf 82
William Lloyd Garrison 83
Oliver Cromwell 83
Charles II 83
Henry Fox 84
George the Fourth 85

Edward Wyllis (E. W.)
    Scripps 85
Nicholas Rubinstein 86
Thomas "Fats" Waller 87
William Sidney Porter (O.
    Henry) 87
H. H. Munro (Saki) 88

Robert Olinger 92
Billy the Kid 92
Pat Garrett 94
Achimedes 95
Arria Paetus 95
Georges Bernanos 96
Marquis B. Stanislas Jean de
    Boufflers 96
Germaine de Staël 96
Ernest Shackleton 97
Henry Stanley 98
Thomas Carlyle 98
Jane Austen 99
John Wolcot 99
William Prescott 99
Thomas Bailey Aldrich 100
Ebenezer Elliott 100
Thurlow Weed 101
Ebenezer Rockwood Hoar 102
Joseph John Gurney 102
Maud Gonne MacBride 102
Lucy Stone 102

Septimius Severus 106
Abd al-Rahman 106

Captain Aristide Dupetit-
Thouars   **107**
Plácido (Gabriel de la
Concepción Valdés)   **107**
John Brown   **108**
James Butler ("Wild Bill")
Hickock   **108**
George Meade   **109**
Thomas J. (Stonewall)
Jackson   **110**
Jay Cooke   **110**
Joan Crawford   **110**
Humphrey Bogart   **111**
Harry Cohn   **112**
Norman Douglas   **113**
A. E. Housman   **113**
Sydney Smith   **114**
William Murphy   **115**
John Holmes   **116**

Lope de Vega   **117**
Henry Ward Beecher   **117**

William Henry Jackson   **120**
John James Audubon   **120**
Arnold Bennett   **121**
Maurice Barrymore   **121**
Eugene O'Neill   **122**
Moe Berg   **123**
Eugene Jacques Bullard   **123**
Katherine Mansfield   **124**
Sir Thomas More   **125**
Charles Dickens   **125**
Anton Chekhov   **126**
Henrik Ibsen   **127**
Arnold Schoenberg   **128**

BIBLIOGRAPHY   **129**

ACKNOWLEDGMENTS

We would like to thank the following people for their assistance during the writing of this book: Jamie Friedman, Lynn Shapiro, Philip Slater, Bennet Fischer, Vincent Solomita, Hilary Nelson, Lisa Schoof, Kathy Trimble and the rest of our families and friends for their patience and encouragement.

Special thanks to Chiyo Ishikawa, our typist; Steven Mikulka for his unfailing interest and numerous leads; and very special thanks to Cynthia Raymond for typing, transportation, accessibility to libraries and her unending moral support.

We would also like to thank the staffs of the libraries at the following schools: Harvard University, Brandeis University, Amherst College, Smith College, Mt. Holyoke College, Hampshire College, Bowdoin College and Palfrey Street School. And public libraries in: Belmont, Cambridge, Watertown, Newton, Northampton, Amherst and Boston, Massachusetts.

Finally, thanks to all the people at E. P. Dutton, especially our editor, Bill Whitehead, whose critical eye and open ear proved invaluable.

S.S. AND A.S.

July 1979

INTRODUCTION

We have received varied responses from our friends when telling them the subject matter of *Exits*. "Sounds morbid," is one of the most common. This is the result of a perfectly understandable mis-understanding. This book is about death, yes, but the emphasis is on people's attitudes toward the inevitable event, rather than physi-cal details or medical analyses. *Exits* is primarily an entertain-ment—and, we feel certain, the most accurate of its kind to date.

Death tends to be a sad event for those staying behind and is popu-larly believed to be pretty sad for the dying person as well. But this book illustrates that death as experienced by the dying person has limitless forms; it can be sad, funny, resigned, angry, painful or joy-ous. In preparing *Exits* we have studied thousands of deaths and have been particularly struck by the large number of people ready to accept, and actually welcome, death. Some of the subjects in this book even tease us with indescribable, light-filled visions of the next phase.

One genuinely depressing truth revealed in *Exits,* however, is the changes in the dying process brought about by twentieth-century technology. Death has changed locale—from the home to the hospital. And the result has been the emergence of a death-denying syndrome in our culture that sociologists have just begun to explore. Technological advances have stripped us of the ability to die with family, friends and dignity.

There has been an interest in the deaths and last words of people, particularly famous ones, since the beginning of recorded history, and probably before. Shakespeare, Bacon, Montaigne, and Addison, among others, took great interest in the subject. A conscious effort to record the last words of dying men and women was a common practice in the days when humans rather than machines were monitoring vital signs. And those words, as you will see, were often valuable. They were observations and comments delivered from a singular vantage point, a vantage point we will all someday share.

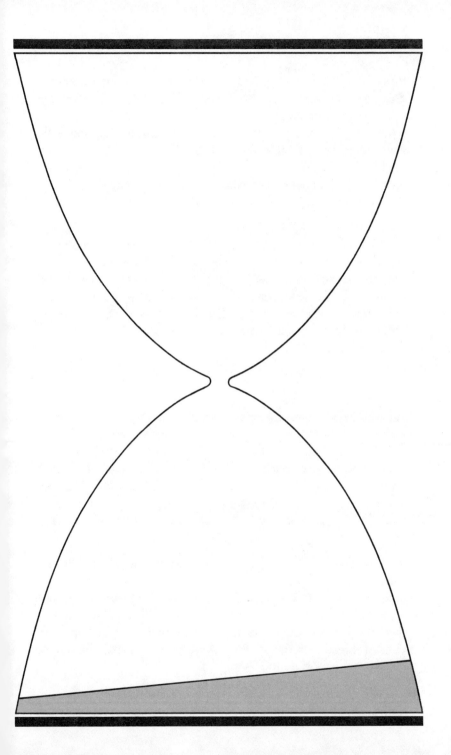

When Merv Griffin asked **Tallulah Bankhead** why she bothered doing his show at the age of sixty-seven after a lifetime of stage and screen stardom she replied, "It's one way of proving to people that I'm not dead." Tallulah, although she severely tested her body with liquor, cocaine and other drugs all her life, outlived most of her friends. On her last visit to London she tried to find old acquaintances in the telephone book with little success. "They're all dead," she said, "and they didn't leave any forwarding addresses."

In December 1968 Tallulah came down with the Asian flu and was forced to enter St. Luke's Hospital in New York, where she made life miserable for the staff by raving against the accommodations and her hospital smock, as well as pulling intravenous needles out of her arm. After a few days she fell into a coma and was placed into a machine that breathed for her. The last discernible words she spoke before dying were, "Codeine . . . bourbon."

☒

Henry David Thoreau spent his last days in Concord, Massachusetts, resting in his parlor, surrounded by family and friends. "Never spent an hour with more satisfaction. Never saw a man dying with so much pleasure and peace," noted Thoreau's former jailer, the tax collector Sam Staples, after a visit. Thoreau was writing, editing and revising ("You know it is the fashion to leave an estate behind you," he said), despite the fact that to do so was an exhausting, nearly impossible chore for him.

Thoreau was aware the end was near; when reminded of this he was invariably good-humored. "It is better some things should end," he told one comforter. During a visit the Quaker abolitionist Parker Pillsbury mused, "You seem so near the brink of the dark river that I almost wonder how the opposite shore may appear to you." Thoreau replied, "My friend, one world at a time." When his

Calvinist Aunt Louisa asked him if he had made his peace with God, Thoreau protested, "I never knew that we had quarreled."

Concord was enjoying a beautiful spring in 1862, the morning of May 6 being no exception. Thoreau's room was filled with flowers, fruits of the season, game, sweetmeats, and get-well messages—the gifts of friends, villagers and even strangers who knew he was ill. Thoreau was deeply touched by these attentions, knowing nature was being brought to him because he could not go into nature. At eight o'clock, as Thoreau lay tossing and turning in this room he murmured his last words—"Moose . . . Indian."

X

Dominique Bouhours, a highly respected French grammarian, was, perhaps, overly dedicated to his profession. He died in 1702 at the age of seventy-four. His last words were, "I am about to—or I am going to—die: either expression is correct."

X

French-born **Henry Labouchere** became one of Britain's leading nineteenth-century statesmen. He was past eighty when he died on January 15, 1912. The afternoon before his death he slept while a friend sat by him. An alcohol burner at his bedside was producing eucalyptus fumes to assist his breathing. The friend accidentally knocked over the burner, waking Labouchere. On seeing the little fire, which was quickly smothered, Labouchere spoke his final words: "Flames? Not yet, I think," and fell back to sleep.

X

Of all the thousands of people who have, over the years, faced the executioner's ax, few have faced it with the calm and courage which **Sir Walter Raleigh** displayed when he was beheaded for treason on October 29, 1618. It is said that Raleigh was the most relaxed man on the scene as he approached the scaffold. He spoke to the crowd before the end, listing the charges against him and illustrating their flimsiness. Raleigh then asked the spectators to pray for his soul.

After taking his gown off the soldier-explorer requested the executioner to show him the ax; when he hesitated, Raleigh said, "I pray thee let me see it. Dost thou think I am afraid of it?" Running his hand along the blade, he commented, "This is a sharp medicine, but it is a physician for all diseases." The executioner knelt and begged his forgiveness; Raleigh comforted him, placing his hands on the man's shoulders, and said, "When I stretch forth my hands, dispatch me." He then lay down and, after a few moments of prayer, stretched his arms out. Unnerved, the executioner could not strike. Raleigh again stretched out his hands. After a moment Raleigh cried out, "Strike, man, strike!" The man struck two blows and it was over.

⧗

In the early morning hours of June 28, 1861, **Elizabeth Barrett Browning** lay dying in bed beside her husband. Her condition had seemed improved the night before, so at 3:00 A.M., when Robert Browning, alarmed that his wife's hands and feet were cold, sent for hot water, Elizabeth said, "Well, you do make an exaggerated case of it." She then kissed her husband over and over, saying, "God bless you," repeatedly. He asked her how she felt and she replied, "Beautiful!" and fell asleep. When she died moments later, her face looked so young and radiant that, for hours, her husband could not persuade himself she was really gone.

4

X

On March 23, 1827, **Ludwig van Beethoven** signed his will with a shaky hand and turned to the visitors by his bedside, saying, "Applaud, friends, the comedy is finished." The fifty-seven-year-old composer was to die the next day. He lay in silence through the night and the following morning, until, on the afternoon of March 24 he was given a gift of wine. He said, "Pity, pity—too late." It was his last utterance; he lapsed into unconsciousness soon after.

Later on in the afternoon a violent thunderstorm began with a brilliant flash of lightning and a loud crack of thunder. Beethoven, responding to the stimuli, rose in his bed, wide-eyed, and lifted his right hand in a clenched fist. He remained in this position for several moments, then fell back, dead.

X

In 1911 the composer **Gustav Mahler** spent the last days of his life in a Vienna sanitarium, surrounded by family, friends, and flowers "from my dear [Vienna] Philharmonic," as he said repeatedly in his more lucid moments. There were not to be many more. Mahler asked, "Who is that strange lady?" when his sister visited, causing her to flee the room. During his last conscious moments a smiling Mahler was moving his fingers, conducting an imaginary orchestra, and murmuring, "Little Mozart, little Mozart."

X

Huddie Ledbetter (Leadbelly), nicknamed "King of the Twelve-String Guitar," was born around 1885 in Louisiana cotton country to a dirt-poor family. Leadbelly's rise to stardom after a life of poverty and violence (which included two prison stretches—one for murder) was phenomenal. His fame, however, did not last long. The writer of the songs "Irene" (later: "Good Night, Irene"), "Midnight Special," and "The Rock Island Line" lived to be sixty-two, forgotten by all but his most faithful followers.

On December 5, 1949, Leadbelly's wife Martha visited him at Bellevue Hospital in New York City, where he lay on the bed, suffering from polio, weakly strumming his guitar. Leadbelly spoke to his wife in disconnected sentences; at one point he said, "You remember 'Careless Love?'" and played some of that song. After a while his doctor entered the room and said, "Mr. Ledbetter, you've got to put your guitar down now. You have to get some sleep." Leadbelly answered, "Doctor, if I put this here guitar down now, I ain't never gonna wake up." He was correct.

⧖

The distinguished actress **Ethel Barrymore** lived to be eighty years of age, and only the fact that she was confined to bed (a victim of rheumatory arthritis and a heart condition) for the last eighteen months of her life prevented her from performing. A frequent visitor during these last months was her fervent admirer, Katherine Hepburn. Hepburn remembers Ethel as "always very well-groomed, and her dark hair well-fixed. I would sit by her side and be thrilled by just the sight of her—that exquisite skin and those beautiful eyes. She always lay among silk bedsheets, and the bed cover was always filled with books. And around the bed were tables, all filled with books."

On a June evening in 1959, Ethel lay asleep in her bed. She suddenly awoke, drew her nurse to her, and asked, "Is everybody happy? I want everyone to be happy. I know I'm happy." Moments later she fell asleep, never to awake again.

☒

Poet **Hart Crane** and his bride-to-be Peggy Robson were on the second leg of their journey to the United States from Mexico in 1932 when he killed himself by jumping overboard the ship *Orizaba.* His stay in Mexico had been tumultuous; he drank heavily, brawled in barrooms more than once and landed in a Mexican jail. The thirty-two-year-old Crane was frantic about lack of money, guilt-ridden about his bisexuality and despairing over what he considered to be his failure as a poet.

As soon as he arrived back on the *Orizaba,* after a layover in Havana, Crane began to drink. The night of April 26 was riotous. He caused such a stir on board he was brought to his room and his door was nailed shut. He escaped somehow and caroused with some sailors until three o'clock in the morning. The "party" concluded with Crane being beaten and robbed. At 3:30 A.M. on April 27 Crane climbed onto the deck railing. The night watchman saw him and dragged him off, and again he was confined to his cabin. The next morning he breakfasted with Peggy Robson and said to her at one point, "I'm not going to make it, dear. I'm utterly disgraced."

At noon Crane, drunk again, was seen hurrying on deck wearing pajamas and an overcoat. He threw off the coat, climbed quickly onto the rail and jumped. Some witnesses claim to have heard him say, "Goodbye, everybody." His body was never found.

☒

Not long before his death, the ninety-one-year-old phenomenon **Pablo Picasso** said to a friend, "Death holds no fear for me. It has a kind of beauty. What I am afraid of is falling ill and not being able to work. That's lost time." The illness and impotence Picasso feared never materialized.

The evening before his death in 1973 Picasso and his wife entertained friends. It was a spirited dinner and Picasso a cheerful, genial host. After the meal, while pouring wine into a friend's glass, Picasso said, "Drink to me. Drink to my health. You know I can't drink any more." A little later, about 11:30 P.M., he left his guests, saying, "And now I must go back to work." He was up painting until 3:00 A.M. That morning Picasso woke at 11:30, unable to move. By 11:40 he was dead.

Χ

Reformer, politician, businessman **Abram Hewitt** made his own decisions. On Sunday, January 18, 1903, Hewitt lay on his hospital bed surrounded by his doctors, wife and children; an oxygen tube was in his mouth sustaining him as he grew weaker. After comforting his family Hewitt took the tube from his mouth, smiled and said, "And now, I am officially dead." And, in fact, he was.

Χ

At the age of seventy-two **Dr. Joseph Henry Green,** the renowned nineteenth-century anatomist turned philosopher, lay on his bed monitoring his own vital signs. His finger was on his wrist, feeling his pulse growing weaker and weaker. He looked up at the doctor by his bedside and said, "Stopped." He was not mistaken; he died that instant.

X

The Emperor **Nero** was a vacillating, procrastinating, pleasure-loving man who moved too slowly to save his own skin. During the spring of A.D. 68 some of the armies of the Roman Empire began to revolt against Nero's rule. When news of the rebellion reached the emperor he reacted by not acting. Instead of addressing his Senate or his people to take measures to defend his regime, Nero went to the theater and played with a new hydraulic-powered organ he owned. His behavior caused dismay among his supporters and a belief that the man was not entirely sane.

In June Nero received a report that additional armies had turned against him and were advancing on Rome. He decided to make a getaway. He ordered a fleet to meet him in Ostia where he would set sail to Egypt. Nero then traveled a little way to his mansion in the Servillian Gardens and took a nap. On awakening, the young ruler found that his guards had deserted him while he slept. He made a round of his friends' homes but no doors would open to him.

Back at the mansion he found his rooms robbed (even of his vial of poison) and most of his servants gone. Fearful of the tortures he would receive if captured, Nero sent the few remaining servants out to find a gladiator to kill him. They returned empty-handed. Nero cried out, "Have I neither a friend nor an enemy?" and rushed to the Tiber River to throw himself in.

On the banks of the river Nero had second thoughts. He decided to find a hiding place. With his three remaining servants he rode out to a friend's country home. The men crawled through some bushes and into the basement of the house. Unfortunately, they had been spotted on the road and his friends urged Nero to take his own life rather than be tortured. Still not quite ready to go, he ordered them

9

to dig a grave first, which he measured with his body. During the digging the singing Emperor kept repeating, "What a loss I shall be to the arts!"

A runner appeared with a letter from the Senate declaring Nero a public enemy and adding that he would be executed "ancient style." Nero asked what was meant by "ancient style," and was told that the victim was stripped, thrust head-first into a wooden fork and flogged to death. Horrified, he picked up two daggers and held them at his throat, but again could not go through with it. He asked if one of the others would commit suicide so he could see how it was done. They declined. Nero whined about his own lack of courage, saying, "This is disgraceful! It is not seemly, Nero!—it is not seemly. One ought to be brave in a situation like this. Come: courage, man!"

The approaching cavalry was now audible and Nero quoted a line from the *Iliad*, "The noise of swift-footed steeds assails my ears." Again he put the daggers to his throat; again he could not do it. One of the men with him clasped the daggers with the Emperor and together they plunged them into Nero's throat. A moment later a centurion entered and tried to stanch the flow of blood (his orders were to take him alive). Nero spoke his last words. "Too late," he said, adding sarcastically, "how *loyal* you are."

⏣

Kusakábé, Japanese political dissident imprisoned in Yeddo in 1859, spoke often with Yoshida-Torajiro, the prisoner in the next cell, as they awaited trial and judgment. The two rebels shared the same passion and the same hopes for their native country, and became close friends during their short time together. Kusakábé was sentenced first and the spot picked for his execution was directly under his friend's window. Kusakábé dared not turn his head toward the window but he did catch Yoshida's eye and said goodbye by quoting the following Chinese verses:

It is better to be a crystal and be broken,
Than to remain perfect like a tile upon the housetop.

X

Charles Darwin suffered from heart trouble in his last years and he died after an attack on April 19, 1882, twenty-three years after the publication of *On the Origin of Species.* His final recorded words, spoken to his son in one of his last conscious moments, were: "I am not the least afraid to die."

X

Missionary to the Massachusetts Indian tribes, **John Eliot** wrote in his journal in 1687, "In y yeare my ancient dearly beloved wife dyed, I was sick to death. but the Lord was pleased to delay me. . . ." He was delayed for only three years, for in 1690, at the age of eighty-six, he joined his wife and four of his sons. The last words he spoke were, "Welcome joy."

X

Eleanor Morehead, wife to **John Morehead,** died on May 29, 1936, after a long illness. John Morehead was a distinguished cleric, teacher and one of the founders of the Lutheran World Convention movement. Morehead was himself too ill to attend his beloved wife's burial. "Will you do me a favor?" he asked his nurse. "Will you kindly ask my physician how long before I shall join my Nellie?" There is no record of the nurse's reply. Morehead joined his Nellie just three hours later.

☒

In the fall of 1953, on his third lecture tour of the U.S., **Dylan Thomas** was in New York City, a long way from the "heron-priested shores" of his boyhood Wales. His last reading, given the day after his thirty-ninth birthday, took place at the City College of New York on October 29. He may, on this occasion, have performed his poem, "And Death Shall Have No Dominion." He almost certainly read, "Do Not Go Gentle into That Good Night," his most popular poem.

For the next three days Thomas was drinking heavily. He spent Tuesday, November 3, in his room at the Chelsea Hotel drinking Old Grandad with the maid and any friends who dropped by. At 2:00 A.M. he got up and went out. When he returned an hour and a half later Thomas said, "I've had eighteen straight whiskeys; I think that's the record." Then to his lover, Liz Reitel, "I love you, but I'm alone." Then he fell asleep.

The following day Thomas was ill with an attack of gastritis and gout. A doctor was called for three times during the course of the day. After Dr. Feldenstein's second visit, Thomas began to hallucinate. He was seeing, "not animals . . . abstractions," geometric shapes. The doctor was summoned a third time and he injected Thomas with half a grain of morphine. There is no known medical reason for administering morphine for gastritis and gout, and even in appropriate circumstances a half-grain dosage would be excessive.

Thomas woke a few times from his morphia-induced sleep. To distract him from his own "horrors" Liz talked about a friend who, when suffering from the dt's, saw "white mice and roses." Thomas said, "Roses plural or Rose's roses with an apostrophe?" Soon after he lapsed into a coma from which he never awoke.

X

The blind Irish bard **Turlough Carolan** was very fond of spirits, especially his native usquebaugh. Carolan's physicians warned him that if he did not abstain he surely would kill himself, but he was unable to stop drinking. In 1738 on his deathbed, moments before the end, he ordered a bowl. His friends tried to dissuade him but he persisted, and when the drink was brought he could not swallow but only wet his lips. "It would be hard," he said, "if two such friends should part at least without kissing." He died a moment later.

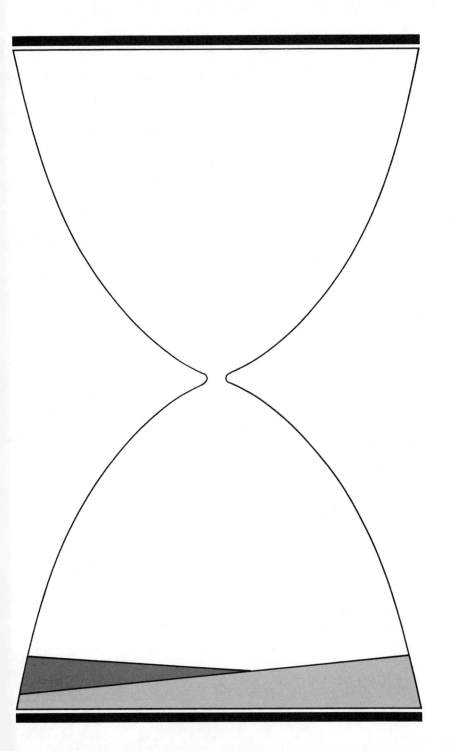

In the winter of 1923 **Sarah Bernhardt,** possibly the most famous actress in history, suddenly slipped into unconsciousness while making up for a dress rehearsal. On awakening an hour later her first words were, "When do I go on?" But she was never to perform again. The seventy-eight-year-old Bernhardt was exhausted. After this collapse the actress was confined to bed for a month, until, feeling somewhat stronger, she was able to get up and move about a bit.

But on March 21 she collapsed again. On March 25, after being informed that there were reporters waiting outside, Madame Sarah said, "All my life reporters have tormented me enough. I can tease them now a little by making them cool their heels." Those were her last words. She died the next day.

$$\text{X}$$

Actor **Paul Muni** was born into the business. In the early years of this century his parents emigrated from Austria (where they were traveling players) to London and then to New York, where they opened their own theater. The young boy would frequently act the parts of elderly men, which he did with astonishing accuracy. His parents were critical of their son's talent; his mother, particularly, had no faith in his acting ability. But Muni persevered and his popularity in the New York Yiddish theater world grew.

At one point in those early years Muni had a conversation with his father who had awakened very late one night and heard his son pacing their apartment. His father asked him what was wrong. Muni said, "Papa, I'm hungry." His father suggested he eat something; Muni suggested his hunger was of a different sort. His father asked if he was hungry for money or fame. The answer was, "I want to be better."

In the years that followed Muni worked in radio and television and starred in twelve Broadway plays and twenty-three movies. He is considered by many to have been the greatest character actor in motion picture history.

Muni died at the age of seventy-two. He had spent his last years watching TV and reading philosophy. In the summer of 1967 he was confined to the hospital, his heart failing. His wife Bella hung pictures of Muni's parents near his hospital bed. On seeing them the actor said, "Take her away." His mother's picture was removed. A picture of his father remained.

On August 25 Bella was sitting by the beside when Muni began moaning. "Are you in pain?" she asked. Muni answered, "Sure. What else is new?" A moment later she heard him whisper to himself, "Munya, be a *mensch*." Alarmed, Bella went off to get a nurse. Evening was falling and, on entering the room, one of the nurses switched on the light. Muni opened his eyes and addressed the photograph of his father. He said, "Papa, I'm hungry." They were his last words.

⧗

The beautiful, talented, intelligent and witty actress **Georgiana Drew** became the wife of the matinee idol Maurice Barrymore, after a courtship that has been described as "a continual bombardment of wit, clever queries and answers which are classics." Their offspring became the most famous theatrical siblings of the age— Ethel, John and Lionel Barrymore. Thirteen-year-old Ethel was Georgie's companion and nursemaid during the last days of her mother's life. In 1893 the mother and daughter were staying in Santa Barbara, California, in the hope that the weather would improve Georgie's ever-worsening health. The weather on July 12 was beautiful, and Georgie spent her Sunday afternoon riding out to visit an old monastery with the mayor of Santa Barbara and his family. On the return journey Georgie began to hemorrhage (she was consumptive). On reaching their destination, the mayor's daughter was sent to fetch Ethel. Georgie died moments after her daughter reached her bedside. Her last words were, "Oh my poor kids. What will ever become of them?"

X

On the afternoon of December 4, 1791, the sick, bedridden composer **Wolfgang Amadeus Mozart** sang with some friends a part of the *Requiem* on which the ex-prodigy had lately been working. The singing stopped when Mozart burst into tears. When Mozart's sister-in-law, Sophie, visited later that day he said to her, "I am glad you are here; stay with me tonight and see me die." Although it was true that Mozart had been very ill for weeks, Sophie was not convinced that death was so near. To her arguments Mozart responded, "I have the flavor of death on my tongue—I taste death. And who will support my dearest Constanze [Mozart's wife], if you do not stay with her."

Thoroughly alarmed, Sophie went to fetch a priest. After she'd gotten one to promise to visit later, she returned. On entering the room she found Mozart lying on his bed with sheets from his *Requiem* scattered all about him. He said to Sophie, "Did I not tell you I was writing the *Requiem* for myself?" Mozart died at one o'clock that night. He was thirty-five years old.

X

One evening in October 1849 Delphine Pototska was singing Stradella's "Hymn to the Virgin" to her dear friend the composer **Frédéric Chopin.** She was interrupted when Chopin burst into one of his increasingly frequent coughing attacks. Confined to his bed in the Place Vendome in Paris, Chopin, stricken with tuberculosis of the lungs and larynx, was suffering horribly from almost incessant, violent coughing. By October 16 Chopin must have realized that the end was near, as he made a request made by many artists on their deathbeds—that his personal papers be destroyed, and that none of his unpublished work be published posthumously. (As in the cases of most artists, these requests were ignored.)

At 11:00 that night Chopin's physician, Dr. Cruveilhier, was taking his pulse. Chopin grabbed his hand away, saying, "It is not worth the trouble, Doctor—soon I'll be rid of you." Sleeping fitfully, coughing spasmodically, Chopin awoke a little past midnight, shouting, "Mother, my poor mother!" He then lay quiet, barely moving. Doctor Cruveilhier bent over Chopin, asking him if he was still in pain. "No more," breathed Chopin, dying almost instantly. In accordance with his wishes, Mozart's *Requiem* was performed at his funeral. It was the first time the *Requiem* had been heard in Paris since Napoleon's body had been brought back from St. Helena in 1821.

X

On April 29, 1821, the former emperor, now exiled political prisoner **Napoleon Bonaparte,** remarked, "I feel so wonderfully well now; I could go for a thirty-mile drive." Within twenty-four hours he was in the throes of a delirium that was to last five days, until his death. The prematurely aging, nearly insane fifty-two-year-old Bonaparte had spent the last six years on the island of St. Helena attended to by a few squabbling friends and officials.

An intensely painful gastric ulcer was the cause of his last illness. There were a few lucid moments for Napoleon in those final few days, but most of his speech consisted of ramblings unfettered by

19

the guides of logic or chronology. He spoke of his Corsican boyhood, and of his one love, his ex-wife Josephine. Reliving his old battles he would cry out, "Quick—forward! Victory is ours; we have them," and call to his generals by name.

The last night was one of excruciating pain and in the early morning hours Napoleon weakly murmured his final words, "France . . . Army! . . . Head of the army! . . . Josephine." Almost immediately after speaking he leapt blindly out of bed, grabbed his friend Montholon, who was standing at the bedside, and wrestled him to the floor. Napoleon's hysterical deathbed grip was so fierce Montholon could not escape it unaided. Another of Napoleon's faithfuls rushed into the room and released him. Bonaparte lay quietly for the rest of the day, and at 5:00 P.M. he died.

☒

Sam Houston and a band of ragged volunteers won "the eighth decisive battle of the world's history" by beating the better-trained and larger Mexican army led by Santa Anna. The battle made Texas a republic and Sam Houston became its president. Houston lived to see Texas become part of the United States, to his great joy, and then secede from same, to his great sorrow. He died in 1863 during the Civil War which he hated. His wife, Margaret, was at his bedside when he stirred and spoke his last words, "Texas—Texas—Margaret."

☒

Otto von Bismarck (1815—98), rose from relatively humble origins to become the most powerful man in Germany, largely responsible for the creation of the German Empire in 1871. The Iron

Chancellor, as he came to be known, fell from power in his later years because of disagreements with William II, for whom he served as Chancellor of the Reich for twenty-one months.

In 1898 Bismarck developed an inflammation of the lungs. He lived for several weeks until July 30 when, flanked by his family, he died. Bismarck muttered incoherently during his last night. At one point he gathered all his strength, grabbed a glass of juice by his bed, drank it, yelled "Forward!" and sank back, never to speak again. He died at eleven that night.

X

Prime Minister of England, **William Pitt,** cried out, "Hear, hear!" a number of times as he lay dying, as if he were still presiding over the House of Commons. A victim of typhoid, the forty-six-year-old Pitt sank rapidly during the last few days of his life despite intense efforts to save him. He spoke little during his final days and when he did it was in a tremulous, high voice dramatically different from the deep, persuasive cadences for which he was famous. Next to the Prime Minister's bed sat Pitt's close friend, the Honorable James H. Stanhope.

At about 3:30 on the morning of Wednesday, January 23, 1806, after a long (and for Stanhope, frightening) silence, Pitt said in clearer tones than he had used for weeks, "Oh my country! How I love my country!" and then fell into a silence which lasted until 4:30 when he quietly slipped into a rather more permanent one.

X

On the morning of October 2, 1780, **John André,** Adjutant-General to the British army, was led from his room in General

George Washington's camp to be executed as a spy. Benedict Arnold, his co-conspirator, was safe miles away behind British lines. The procession to the execution site was very melancholy; the intelligent, talented, charming André had completely endeared himself to his American captors including Lafayette and Washington himself. Washington, who, under the rules of war, not only had to execute but also to hang André, was deeply tormented. André had repeatedly requested to be shot rather than hanged and indeed was under the impression that his request was to be granted as he walked toward the gallows.

As the hanging-tree came into his sight, André reeled and looked to his escort. "Why this emotion, sir?" one asked. "I am reconciled to my fate," said André, his fists clenched, "but not to the mode of it." A guard murmured, "It is unavoidable, sir." André then appealed to an officer he knew: "Must I then die in this manner?" Told that it was the order, he said, "How hard is my fate, but it will soon be over."

Upon reaching the gibbet itself, André displayed open disgust toward the method of his impending execution. After climbing up onto the wagon, he jerked open his collar, grabbed the noose from the hangman and fastened it tightly around his own neck, the knot under his right ear. André then blindfolded himself with his own handkerchief, listened as the order of execution was read, and was told he might speak: "All I request of you, gentlemen, is that you will bear witness to the world that I die like a brave man." Then, turning aside, he softly said, "It will be but a momentary pang." An officer ordered André's arms bound behind his back, this done with a second handkerchief which André offered. The height of the tree, the length of the rope, and sudden drawing of the wagon from under his feet all conspired to kill André instantly.

$$\boxtimes$$

X

At the age of sixty-seven **George Washington** still rode out every day and made the rounds of his estate. The morning of December 12, 1799, was chilly and overcast. It began to snow at about one o'clock when Washington was in the middle of his tour. The snow turned first to hail, then to a cold rain. Washington returned at three and ate dinner without changing his clothes. The next day the ex-president stayed inside with a sore throat and that night became very ill and had great difficulty breathing.

Doctors, summoned early on the morning of December 14, tried several remedies (including bleeding) but to no avail; the president was steadily weakening. Breathing was extremely painful for him and at about five in the afternoon he said to his old friend, Dr. Craik, "I die hard but I am not afraid to go. I believed from my first attack that I should not survive it—my breath cannot last long." A little later he said to his other physicians, "I feel I am going. I thank you for your attentions but I pray you to take no more trouble about me; let me go off quietly; I cannot last long." He died that evening between ten and eleven o'clock.

X

The most famous of German writers, **Johann Wolfgang von Goethe,** was in excellent health for a man of his age (eighty-two) until March 15, 1832, when he caught a cold. Complications ensued and the artist collapsed five days later. He died on March 22, ringed by friends and the remaining members of his family.

Several times before dying Goethe stirred in his sleep and spoke various disconnected phrases, at one point crying out passionately,

"Light! Light! More light!" An hour after this outburst he said his last words to his daughter, Ottilie, "Come my little one, and give me your little hand." Goethe spoke no more, but in his last moments he raised his hand and scrawled figures and letters on the air with his forefinger and, when he could hold his hand up no longer, on the shawl that covered him.

☒

On May 22, 1885, 5,000 people were gathered on L'avenue **Victor Hugo** outside the house of one of the most celebrated writers in history. The man who received mail addressed:

Victor Hugo
on his own street, Paris

was inside dying at the age of eighty-three. Hugo had fallen ill on May 15. The condition became aggravated with the onset of pneumonia and by May 22 he knew death was very near. He spent his last day saying goodbye to friends and family. (Juliet Drouet, his lover for over half a century, had died in Hugo's arms two years earlier.) To Paul Meurice, a close friend, he said, "Death will be very welcome." A few hours later, before slipping into a coma, Hugo said softly, "I see black light." He never regained consciousness.

☒

Augustus Bozzi Granville, sailor, doctor and Italian patriot, died at the age of eighty-eight, his daughter by his side. He had been confined to bed for a painful eight weeks in 1872 before the Sunday when he bent over and whispered in his daughter's ear, "Light. All light," before falling asleep for the last time.

X

Sir Walter Scott wrote lovingly in his memoirs and correspondence about his old schoolteacher, **Dr. Alexander Adam.** Adam was totally committed to his boys and remembered how each of his students performed in his class as well as where they ended up in later years. While teaching a class in 1809 Adam suffered an attack of palsy.

For a few days he clung to life. He became delirious on this last day and, after a silence lasting several hours, died immediately after speaking the words, "That Horace was very well said; *you* did not do it so well. But it grows dark, very dark—*the boys may dismiss.*"

X

The beloved German poet **Heinrich Heine** died in February 1856 at the age of fifty-eight. He suffered terribly in the last years of his life as a result of the syphilis he had contracted as a youth. But his almost supernatural sense of humor never left him. When visitors asked him, "Are you really incurable?" he replied, "Oh no, I'll die someday."

Someone suggested that his illness was a consequence of excessive work. Heine reportedly answered, "Well, it was *excess* at any rate." One visitor was told, upon entering Heine's room, "Ah, you find me utterly stupid." "You mean ill?" said the visitor. "No, stupid," said Heine. "You see, Alexander Weill was just here, and we exchanged ideas."

At the very end his suffering increased and prompted Heine to say that he was considering reporting God to the Society for the Prevention of Cruelty to Animals. One or two days before his death as Heine's wife sat by him praying for his soul, the poet said, "God will forgive me—that's his job." Heine died on February 15, 1856, a Sunday afternoon. The nurse by his side heard him murmur, "write, write," to which she replied calmingly, "Yes, yes." Suddenly he sat up in his bed and ordered, "Pencil—paper." As the nurse hurriedly put a pencil in his paralyzed hand, Heine fell back, dead.

X

Producer and screenwriter **Herman Mankiewicz** had no scarcity of visitors on his last day on earth. Hospitalized in April of 1953, the writer of *Citizen Kane, Girl Crazy, Dinner at Eight* and other witty, topical screenplays, was suffering from edema and the doctors had given up hope. The numerous members of his family had traveled from around the country to be by Herman's side during his final days and hours.

When his brother Frank walked in the room in a brand-new, dark blue suit, Herman said, "That's a very bad sign. Your suit is much too black and absolutely appropriate for a funeral." And to another sibling, Don, Mankiewicz actually discussed details of his funeral, saying, "Assuming the ceremony will be held indoors, hats will not be worn. You won't have any trouble, except that Dore Schary will wear his hat. You are to go up to Dore Schary and tap him on the shoulder and say, 'Dore, I have a message for you from the deceased: Take off your hat, you're in the house.' "

Other relatives and friends came in and the hospital room was becoming so airless that Mankiewicz requested they each visit one by one. At one point a rabbi entered the room to provide solace. Mankiewicz threw him out immediately, yelling, "Get the hell out of here. I never had any use for you when I was living and I've got no use for you now."

Herman's last visitor was his brother Joe, with whom he'd had a painful love-hate (mostly hate) relationship for years. They had squabbled both personally and professionally. They had worked on films together, and, more than once, were co-makers on Morris Plan loans. Their conversation was brief but apparently more satisfying than any they'd had in years. As Joe left, Herman made his last joke. "Well that finishes everything I've got to take care of before I go to meet my maker. Or in my case, should I say 'co-maker'?"

Later when Mankiewicz slipped into a coma the nurse went out to tell Sara, his wife. Sara came into the room, approached her husband, and, gripping his shoulders, shook him in an attempt to bring him back. She put her mouth to his ear and called his name. With a sudden, strong movement he pushed her away but did not wake. Sara said later, "Whatever he was doing or thinking, or wherever he was going, he did not want to be interrupted."

X

Florenz Ziegfeld's last show took place in 1932 in his room at the Cedars of Lebanon Hospital in Las Vegas. Sidney, his valet and confidential secretary, was at the producer's bedside when Ziegfeld, consumed with fever, suddenly sat up and went to work. "Let the curtain go up," he ordered, "and I want some fast music." Deciding to humor his boss, Sidney turned on the radio. ". . . What is that tall girl doing on the end? She doesn't belong here at all," said Ziegfeld. His valet explained that the girl was out of work and had a family to support. "All right, let her stay," said Ziegfeld, "We'll find some place for her."

He then imagined a run-through of the comedy portion of the show which he cut off, ". . . All right, boys, you'll have to stop the scene. I want to look at the girls." After requesting brighter lights for the girls, Ziegfeld, with a great effort, pulled himself out of bed and said, "Ready for the finale . . . the seats in this theater ought to be fixed. Who's in the back there, making that noise? Throw him out. This is a dress rehearsal. We're opening tomorrow night. Hurry up. The finale!" Sidney turned the radio to a station with more volume. "That's fine. Go to the bank Sidney. See if that check came in . . . the show looks great!"

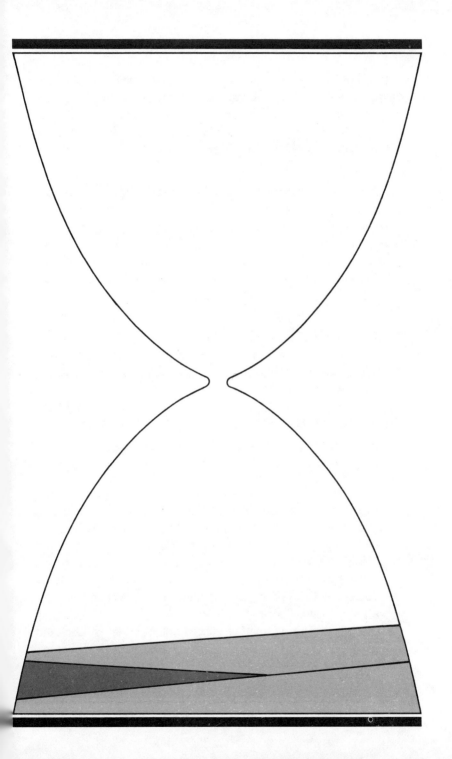

A scene out of countless movies and countless thrillers is that of a dying criminal sneeringly refusing to talk to the law. Some real-life counterparts were equally stubborn, and examples are numerous. A cheap hood and gambler named **Jack Rybakoff,** when asked by the police who had shot him, told them, "Me mudder did the job."

In 1958, **Frank Kierdorf,** a professional arsonist, slipped up and ended in the hospital with burns over 85% of his body. A law enforcement official leaned over the dying man, saying, "You only have a few minutes to live. You are about to meet your maker, your God. Make a clean breast of things; tell me what happened." Kierdorf mumbled something. His inquisitor moved closer, putting his ear to Kierdorf's mouth. "Speak a little louder, if you can, Frank." Kierdorf struggled to speak. "I said . . . go fuck yourself."

The lengthiest and best-documented dying speech belongs to Arthur Flegenheimer, better known as **Dutch Schultz.** After being gunned down in a New Jersey restaurant, Schultz, mortally wounded, was taken to Newark City Hospital, where a police stenographer took down every word of Schultz's delirious ramblings. The date was October 24, 1935. These are the last minutes:

Q: Who shot you? A: I don't know who can have done it. Anybody. Kindly take my shoes off.

Q: They are off. A: No, there is a handcuff on them. The baron says these things. I know what I am doing here with my collection of papers. It isn't worth a nickel to two guys like you and me, but to a collector it is worth a fortune. It is priceless. I am going to turn it over to—turn your back to me, please. Henry. I am so sick now. The police are getting many complaints. Look out. I want that G-note. Look out for Jimmy Valentine, for he's a pal of mine. Come on, come on, Jim. O.K., O.K., I am all through. I can't do another thing. Look out, Mama. Look out for her. You can't beat him. Police, Mama, Helen, mother, please take me out. I will settle the indictment. Come on, open the soap duckets; the chimney sweeps. Talk to the sword. Shut up. You got a big mouth. Please help me get up. Henry! Max! Come over here. French Canadian bean soup. I want to pay. Let them leave me alone."

The stenographer wrote after this last sentence, "Schultz sank into unconsciousness then. It was 6:40 P.M. He died less than two hours later, without saying anything else."

ᛟ

Toward the end of 1943 **Damon Runyon** began to pay attention to a sore throat that had been bothering him for years. The diagnosis was cancer. In April and May of the following year Runyon underwent two operations which involved the removal of his larynx. From then until his death in 1946 the author could communicate only by silently mouthing words and writing notes.

Runyon, novelist, columnist and perhaps America's greatest sports writer, was known as The Gentleman of Broadway. His short stories about the "citizens" of night-time Manhattan (collected in *Guys and Dolls*) are still entertaining reading. After his operations Runyon continued writing his column for the Hearst papers. His awareness of fast-approaching death seemed to mellow the writer and his columns (which had been cynical and bitter of late) became, once again, affirmative and humorous.

Runyon decided he wanted to be cremated and his ashes scattered on Broadway "that my spirit may mingle with the throng here through the years to come and also that I may keep hep to the scandal in my set."

Runyon's closest friend in his later years was Walter Winchell, who wrote in one of his columns in late November of 1946, "Runyon

being ill is like New York Bay—with the Statue of Liberty dark."
Winchell himself was unwell and in Florida, resting, when Runyon
was taken to the hospital for the last time. Anticipating a stubborn
refusal, Runyon's doctors and friends led him to believe he was just
going out for a drive, so when the car pulled up in front of Memo-
rial Hospital, Damon was understandably upset. He mouthed word-
lessly at the entrance, "Where's Walter? Where's Walter? He
wouldn't let you do this to me."

In the hospital Runyon wrote one last note to his friends, "You can
keep the things of bronze and stone, and give me one man to
remember me just once a year."

He fell into a coma on December 7, 1946, and died three days
later.

𐤗

Early Monday morning, November 18, 1946, **Jimmy Walker,** the
celebrated former mayor of New York City, lay in the bedroom of
his East End Avenue apartment, alone except for a nurse. He attempted to rise from his bed, and, despite the protestations of his
nurse, finally did. "Am I not the master of my own house?" Walker
asked. "Yes, Mr. Mayor, but you—" Walker interrupted her: "Oh,
you must be a good Democrat." "Yes, Mr. Mayor, I am," she answered. Walker, always the gentleman, bowed to her and intoned,
"In that case, nurse, I shall abide by the wishes of a fair constitu-
ent." With that he lay back down in his bed, smiling at the nurse.
Suddenly he began breathing fitfully. Shortly thereafter he fell into
a coma, and died later that evening in Doctor's Hospital.

𐤗

When Lord Brougham bumped into his friend Chief Justice **Charles Abbott,** in the early part of 1832 he recognized that the seventy-year-old judge was very ill indeed. He tried to convince Abbott to go home. "Go, Chief Justice," he said. "You will kill yourself." Abbott replied, "It is already done." Later on that year Abbott was presiding over a misconduct trial when his age and illnesses compelled him to hand the matter over to a colleague and retire to his home. The universally respected Abbott had only two weeks to live. His very last words before dying, spoken from a semi-comatose state, were, "Gentlemen, you are all dismissed."

X

When President **William Henry Harrison** died in office of pleurisy his feverish mind was focused on the business of government. After he had been in bed for a week he rallied for a short time and then suffered a relapse. He knew before his doctors that his time had come. "Ah Fanny," he confided to an attendant, "I am ill, very ill, much more so than they think me." After that he fell into a stupor, speaking snatches of unconnected phrases.

On April 4, 1841, he died immediately after firmly delivering the following admonishment to an imaginary adversary: "Sir, I wish you to understand the true principles of government. I wish them carried out. I ask nothing more."

X

In 1830 **John Quincy Adams** accepted the wishes of the people of Plymouth to represent them in Congress. The ex-president served his constituents faithfully and bravely. (It was in his last years that the anti-slavery battles were fought in the House and Senate, and Adams was at the head of the Northern faction. He also struggled against enactment of the measures that led the United States into war with Mexico.)

On February 21, 1848, the House was in session when Adams rose to speak and collapsed, unconscious, into the arms of the congressman next to him. Adams held on to life for two days. On the afternoon of February 23 he was heard to say, "Thanks to the officers of the House." And later on that evening, just before he died, Adams murmured, "This is the last of earth, I am content."

X

Lytton Strachey stood at the head of the Bloomsbury Group of artists, intellectuals and writers who worked in England in and around the 1920s. Author of *Eminent Victorians, Queen Victoria* and *Elizabeth and Essex,* Strachey blasted the prejudices and follies of the age which preceded his own. His wit, economy and sensitivity made him a master of the biographical sketch. Strachey died of stomach cancer on January 21, 1932, in his early fifties. The last words he spoke, just before slipping into unconsciousness, were characteristic: "If this is dying, then I don't think much of it."

X

The young, promising football player **Brian Piccolo** underwent seven agonizing months of operations, chemotherapy and radiotherapy before his death from cancer in June 1970.

On his last day alive his wife Joy was with him in his hospital room when he said to her, "I'm going to lick this. I'm going to get out of here." Then he made an "ok" sign with his thumb and forefinger. A little later Piccolo jerked up to a sitting position, his eyes wide,

and screamed, "Can you believe it, Joy? Can you believe this shit!"
Those were his last words. He died in his sleep three hours later.

X

George Combe, British barrister and enthusiastic champion of the
once-respected "science" of phrenology (or head-reading) was
stricken suddenly in 1858 with respiratory ailments, confined to bed
and died within two weeks. On the day of his death Combe spoke
his last words to the doctor at his bedside: "From my present sensa-
tions, I should say I was dying—and I am glad of it."

X

Élie Metchnikoff, the Russian zoologist, microbiologist and bacte-
riologist, co-winner of the 1908 Nobel Prize for Physiology of Medicine, was very interested in the study of longevity. He felt humans
should live far longer than they usually do, and that if they were
allowed to attain a "normal" age, they would accept dying as the
logical end to a natural cycle, and therefore peacefully and without
fear. Shortly before his death, Metchnikoff proclaimed that "there
will . . . be a new science—the science of death; it will be known
how to make it less hard."

Metchnikoff himself suffered a long illness, his sufferings eased by
constant doses of Pantopon (an opium derivative), by the atten-
tiveness of his wife Olga, and by numerous doctors of the Pasteur
Institute. By July 14, 1916, Metchnikoff was inhaling oxygen
frequently and demanding increased amounts of Pantopon, amid
Olga's protestations that the narcotic would cause prolonged and
deep sleep.

"But an eternal sleep is precisely what I want!" Metchnikoff cried. "Do you understand that now nothing is left to me but Pantopon? What is the good of making me last? Is this a life? A few days or a month have no importance when one is not going to recover. And you cannot wish to prolong my sufferings." The following afternoon as he was inhaling some oxygen he hiccoughed. "It is the end," he told Olga. "The death rattle; that is how people die." He then noted that his watch read four o'clock. "It must have stopped. Four o'clock struck some time ago. Is it not strange that it should have stopped before I? Go and see what time it is." It was 4:40.

Olga grew alarmed at Metchnikoff's forebodings, and sent for one of his doctors. She tried to calm his fears, causing him to remark, "But my child, why do you want to calm me? I am quite calm; I am only stating the facts." At that moment, Dr. Salimbeni arrived. Metchnikoff said, "Salimbeni, you are a friend; tell me, is it the end?" Salimbeni denied that it was. Metchnikoff then asked, "You remember your promise? You will do my post-mortem? And look at the intestines carefully, for I think there is something there now." (He had earlier complained of feeling a heaviness in his intestines.) Metchnikoff then moved suddenly, and died of cardiac failure. The autopsy showed ascites of the peritoneum, an inflammation of membrane lining the abdominal cavity and the organs contained therein, including the large intestine.

$$\rtimes$$

Dr. George Miller Beard (1839–83) made immense contributions to the medical literature of his time, writing on subjects ranging from hay fever and seasickness to the medical use of electricity and the psychology of the Salem witch-hunters. He was instrumental in effecting advances in attitudes toward, and treatment for, the mentally ill.

Even on his deathbed Beard's commitment to investigation and analysis was foremost on his mind. Addressing his visitors, he said, "Tell the doctors it is impossible for me to record the thoughts of a dying man. It would be interesting to do so but I cannot. My time has come. I hope others will carry on my work."

☒

The eloquent Scottish anatomist **William Hunter,** famous for his extensive anatomical and pathological collection, fainted immediately after lecturing on operative surgery on March 20, 1783, in London. The following day, as he lay in bed with a mysterious, undiagnosed paralysis, he discussed his symptoms with his friend and associate Dr. Coombe. Hunter, who had been miserable with the gout for years, said he believed he had suffered a paralytic stroke. Dr. Coombe replied that he thought Hunter might be mistaken, as his pulse and speech were both unaffected. As it turned out, Hunter was correct. The anatomist's last words came ten days later, when, turning to Dr. Coombe, he remarked, "If I had strength enough left to hold a pen, I would write how pleasant and easy a thing it is to die."

☒

On Thursday evening, February 3, 1820, **John Keats** entered his lodgings in Wentworth Place with a high fever and staggering like a drunk. It was immediately clear to his friend, Charles Brown, that Keats was very ill. He sent the poet upstairs to bed. Keats was just getting under the covers when Brown entered the room with a glass of liquor. As he was making himself comfortable Keats coughed softly and said, "That is blood from my mouth." He then said to his friend, "Bring me the candle, Brown, and let me see this blood."

Brown did so. Keats, who had studied medicine before devoting all his energies to poetry, looked at the blood for a moment, turned to Brown and said, "I know the color of that blood; it is arterial blood. I cannot be deceived in that color. That drop of blood is my death warrant. I must die."

His diagnosis of tuberculosis was correct. The twenty-five-year-old Keats was to die the same slow and painful death he had witnessed his brother endure only a year before. During the next year the once vibrant, healthy poet declined physically and also suffered frightening fits of moodiness and depression brought on partially by his illness, partially by some sharp criticism of his early poetry and partially by his intense possessiveness toward his fiancée, Fanny Brawne.

March, April and May of 1820 were relatively calm and reasonably healthy months for Keats, who spent the time resting, being bled, revising some poetry and writing passionate, jealous letters to Miss Brawne. But in June he had a relapse. In his weakened state Keats suffered intermittently from delusions of persecution—on the one hand, blaming his illness on literary critics and on the other, blaming Fanny Brawne, for not sleeping with him.

In August after another severe hemorrhage, it was decided that Keats must travel to Italy for the fall and winter months. The darkly attractive young man, whose charm and sweetness of character had assured him a host of faithful, loving friends, was, by now, bitter and desperate and threatening suicide. A friend who visited him in August said, "[he seems] . . . to be going out of the world with contempt for this and no hopes of the other."

The painter Joseph Severn agreed, on very short notice, to accompany his friend to Italy. They set sail on September 13. The voyage was a nightmare, and more than once Keats begged Severn to allow him to take his own life. From Naples (where the ship was quarantined for a hellish ten days because of a rumor of typhoid) the two men traveled to Rome. There Keats was somewhat calmer and more philosophical. He wrote his last letter to Charles Brown back in England, ending it sadly: "I can scarcely bid you goodbye even in a letter. I always make an awkward bow."

The short calm was broken on December 10 when he again suffered a hemorrhage, frightening in its severity. After the doctor left his bedside Keats staggered about his room crying, "This day shall be my last!" Fortunately (perhaps), Severn had hidden all possible vehicles of self-destruction (knives, forks, drugs) so Keats could not effect his threat. The two months which followed were the saddest and angriest. Keats repeatedly tried to convince Severn to let him die. And every time the doctor visited, Keats asked the same question: "How long is this posthumous life of mine to last?"

Toward the middle of February 1821, Keats relaxed. As he began to accept his death and the life that preceded it, he could see beyond his own plight and begin to appreciate the dedication of his friends, particularly Joseph Severn. He even found the strength to counsel Severn about the coming event. "Now you must be firm," he said, "for it will not last long."

On February 23 at 4:00 P.M. Keats called out, "Severn—Severn—lift me up for I am dying—I shall die easy—don't be frightened—thank God it has come." For the next seven hours Severn held Keats in his arms, their hands clasped. Keats spoke only once more; after suddenly breaking out into a sweat he whispered, "Don't breathe on me—it comes like ice." He died very quietly at 11:00 P.M.

Ⅹ

Charlotte Brontë's last weeks were a dazed half-life during which she slipped into and out of consciousness, gradually becoming more and more remote from those around her. In 1855 a few days before her death she woke, in one of her last lucid moments, to the voice of her husband asking God to spare her life. "Oh," she whispered, "I am not going to die, am I? He will not separate us, we have been so happy."

⚹

On the morning of March 28, 1941, **Virginia Woolf** wrote some letters, one to her sister Vanessa, and two to Leonard, her husband. She then took her walking stick and crossed the meadows to the River Ouse where she put a heavy stone into the pocket of her coat, walked into the river and drowned. In her last letter to Leonard she had written: ". . . I feel I am going mad again. I feel we can't go through another of those terrible times. . . . Everything has gone from me but the certainty of your goodness. I can't go on spoiling your life any longer.

"I don't think two people could have been happier than we have been."

⚹

In 1897 **Barney Barnato,** British speculator, was sailing from South Africa to London with his family. On board he was jovial and talkative, a radical change from the behavior brought on by the intense depression, paranoia and hallucinatory episodes he had lately been experiencing.

At lunch on June 14 Barnato was particularly entertaining and had everyone around him amused. A little later in the afternoon he walked around on deck with his nephew for an hour. Fatigued, Barnato's nephew sank down into a deck chair and invited his uncle to join him. "What's the time?" asked Barnato. "I make it just thirteen minutes past three," was the answer. Suddenly Barnato, as if pursued, sprinted to the ship's railing and leaped into the ocean. His body was recovered, but too late.

X

When **Cecil Rhodes** was twenty-four years old he made the first of seven wills in which he left his as yet un-made fortune to the colonial secretary to found a secret society, "the true aim and object whereof shall be the extension of British rule throughout the world."

After graduating from college, Rhodes went to Africa (where he had spent much of his youth) to exploit the land and people of that continent for diamonds. By 1891 his company, de Beers Consolidated Mines, owned 90% of the diamond production in the world. Rhodes spent the rest of his life making more money and taking more land from the African tribes (as well as the Dutch settlers); Rhodesia is named for Cecil Rhodes. He, perhaps more than any one man, was responsible for establishing British rule in Africa. On his deathbed in 1902 Rhodes's last words were: "So little done. So much to do."

X

Robert S. Brookings, manufacturer, businessman, philanthropist and key contributor to and organizer of the Brookings Institute, died in 1932 after an attack of chills and fever. Brookings had led a life with which he seemed to be satisfied. His last words, spoken to the nurse at his bedside, were, "I have done everything I wanted to do. This is the end."

X

When **John Jacob Astor** died on March 29, 1848, he was the richest man in the United States, worth between twenty and thirty million dollars. Until the age of eighty he was active and alert, still retaining a strong interest in the care and increase of his property. He was not known for his generosity. "This man will never succeed," he grumbled to his friend Joseph Cogswell, referring to the owner of the restaurant in which they were sitting. "Why not, Mr. Astor?" "Don't you see what large lumps of sugar he puts in the bowl?" said Astor.

On another occasion Astor had rented an enormous sailboat. As he and Cogswell strolled toward the pier Cogswell mischievously remarked that every minute Astor had the boat it was costing him twenty-five cents. Astor immediately began running anxiously toward the mooring. After his eightieth birthday in 1843 Astor began to deteriorate physically. Partially paralyzed, stricken with a palsy, he became a drooling, unintelligible old man, his mind more and more occupied with his one obsession—the acquisition of money.

During the last weeks of his life in 1848 his servants would wrap Astor in a blanket and toss him up and down in order to keep his circulation going. One day in the midst of one of these sessions one of Astor's rent collectors walked into the room. The following conversation ensued. Astor screamed at him, "Has Mrs. ———— paid that rent yet?" "No," replied the agent. "Well, but she *must* pay it." "Mr. Astor, she can't pay it now; she has had misfortunes, and we must give her time." Astor was firm. "No, no, I tell you she can pay it, and she *will* pay it. You don't know the right way to work with her."

Exasperated, the agent said his goodbyes and left, informing Astor's son William of his father's demand. William gave the rent collector the money out of his pocket and told him to tell John Jacob that it was the rent. The agent walked back inside and handed Astor the money. "There, I told you that she would pay it if you went the right way to work with her," said Astor. The only nourishment he was able to take in these last weeks was fresh breast milk.

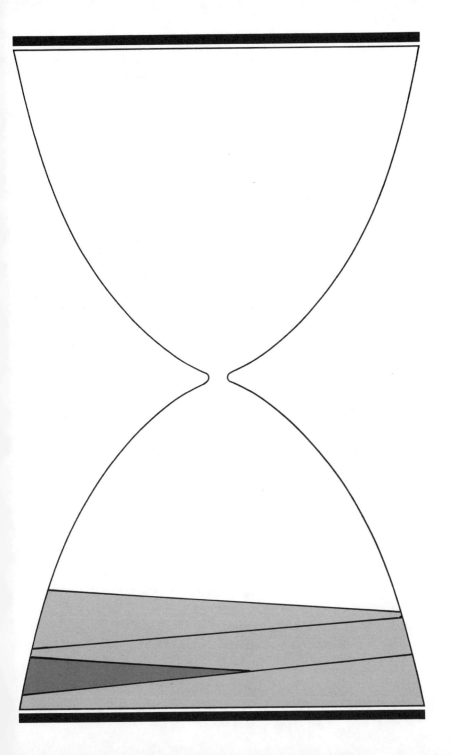

The controversial French sculptor **Auguste Rodin** was married to his mistress of 53 years, Rose Beuret, on January 28, 1917. She was 72 and he was 77. Besides their love they shared an increasing infirmity of mind. Rodin's country estate, Meudon, was in shambles. Rodin in his dotage had been plagued by scores of fortune-hunting females eager for both contact with the great man and a share of his fortune and artistic treasures. Strange men and women moved in and out of Meudon, seemingly at will. Works of art disappeared.

Matters were further complicated by the presence of Rodin's son and daughter-in-law, both alcoholic, and as guilty of plundering as any strangers. Because of wartime coal rationing it was impossible to heat the enormous house properly. The rooms became emptier and emptier as statuary was carted off to the new Rodin Museum, leaving Meudon empty and barren as well as disorganized and cold. The state of France, quick to accept the donation of Rodin's life work and a place to house them, was not so willing to part with enough coal to keep him alive.

Two weeks after their marriage Rose died of bronchial pneumonia. As Rodin viewed his long-suffering wife he said, "How beautiful she is, a piece of sculpture, real sculpture." He was to join her soon. By November Rodin was more or less abandoned in his ice-cold estate. Although his doctor repeatedly warned everyone about the dangers of Rodin living in completely unheated quarters, nothing was done. Everyone was too occupied with the war, with one exception. On November 15 time was found to further adjust Rodin's will, in order to clear up some complications concerning the Rodin Museum. (Witnesses testified that Rodin had wanted to sign, but was unable to do so.)

He lay shivering in his vast, empty house, dispossessed of everything, nearly alone. He died at 4:00 in the morning, November 17, 1917. To the end his thoughts ran to art. "And they say that Puvis de Chavannes's work is not beautiful!'' were his last words. Auguste Rodin had died of the cold.

Ⅹ

Vincent van Gogh was in Auvers, the scene of his brightest, most colorful paintings, when he decided that the madness which had plagued him all his life had become unendurable. He wrote his last letter to his brother Theo ending with the words, ''But what's the use?'' He then walked up a country road and into a field where he pulled out his revolver and shot himself. The gun went off too quickly and the bullet lodged in his stomach. Van Gogh walked back to his room above a cafe where he was discovered minutes later moaning in pain and smoking his pipe. When Theo reached his brother's bedside the next day he asked him why he did it. Van Gogh answered, ''Who could imagine that life could be so sad?''

Van Gogh's last words, spoken just minutes before his death the next morning, were, ''I wish I could die now.''

Ⅹ

French landscape painter **Jean Corot** lived to be seventy-eight years old. He died in 1875, already recognized, revered and loved as a great master. Corot was staring at the ceiling as he spoke his dying words, ''How beautiful it is! I have never seen such beautiful landscapes.''

Ⅹ

Thomas Edison died on October 18, 1931, at the age of eighty-four, after lying in a coma for five days. Just before he went under,

Edison looked out of his bedroom window across the valley by his home and said, "It is very beautiful over there."

⅄

The writer **Stephen Crane** died of tuberculosis in 1900 at the age of twenty-eight. Not long before his death Crane was visited by his friend Robert Barr, to whom he gave a glimpse of the places he was visiting in his delirium. "Robert—when you come to the hedge—that we must all go over, it isn't bad. You feel sleepy—and—you don't care. Just a little dreamy anxiety which world you're in—that's all."

⅄

Poet **William Allingham** died on November 18, 1889. He was asked on the day before if he had any requests to make. He said, "No, my mind is at rest," then turned to his wife and quoted from his own "Poet's Epitaph":

"And so, to where I wait, come gently on."

For the rest of the time until his death Allingham lay in a trancelike state from which he roused himself once to say, "I am seeing things that you know nothing of."

⅄

Aldous Huxley, the most famous of the brilliant, accomplished Huxleys, author of *Brave New World* and dozens of other volumes, and advocate of the perceptual and intellectual insights gained from the use of hallucinogens, died on November 22, 1963, of cancer.

46

Huxley faced his coming death much the same way he faced life: with curiosity, objectivity and gentleness.

Working to the last, Huxley spent his closing days dictating an article on Shakespeare to his wife Laura. By the morning of November 22 his condition was grave. His breathing became agitated, forcing him to alternate between verbal and written communication. Toward noon he wrote a note to his wife:

LSD—try it intermuscular—100 mm—

Laura conferred with Huxley's doctor and then gave her husband the injection. About two hours later she administered another one. Huxley was silent, awake and appeared to be relieved and peaceful for the next few hours. He died just after 5:00 P.M.

X

Artist, craftsman, poet and socialist **William Morris** died in 1896 at the age of sixty-two. Morris was a man concerned with beauty and simplicity; his advances in the visual arts were considerable and his socialism was based on the ideals of love and harmony. He was a practical romantic who believed the world could be altered for the better. Almost his very last utterance as he lay dying was, "I want to get mumbo jumbo out of the world."

X

George Bernard Shaw died on November 2, 1950, at the age of ninety-four. The literary giant whose life spanned a century and whose work spans the ages was tired, though still lucid, during his last days. In his later years he had confided to a few close friends that he was ready, if not longing, for his final rest.

On his last day alive Shaw was visited by a friend, Ellen O'Casey. At one point he turned to her and said wryly, "Well, it will be a new experience anyway." He died an hour later.

X

Playwright, theatrical innovator, fascist and Nobel prizewinner, **Luigi Pirandello** died on December 15, 1936, at the age of sixty-nine. Pirandello's very last words go unrecorded. Just a few days before the end, however, his doctor stood over his deathbed and tried to cheer him up with white lies about his condition. Never one to shirk his truth and committed at the last to the precise use of language, Pirandello said, "No need to be so scared of words, doctor. This is called dying."

X

At the age of fifty-six **Alexander Pope**'s fragile body was giving out, though his mind was nearly as focused as ever. Under the dubious care of Dr. Thompson, a notorious quack, Pope's last few weeks were spent writing and talking to friends. He was sending out copies of a new edition of his "Moral Epistles" to various acquaintances. About the gifts he said he was ". . . like Socrates distributing my morality among my friends just as I am dying." When his doctor assured Pope he was better, Pope said, with a strong pulse and less labored breathing, "Here I am, dying of a hundred good symptoms." Pope died soon after on May 30, 1744, so quietly that those around his bedside were unable to pinpoint the time of death.

X

In ancient Greece the customary form of execution was to have the condemned man drink, on the appointed day, a glass of poison. **Socrates** was surrounded by his friends when his time came in 399 B.C. Before killing himself he bathed to avoid "giving the women the trouble of washing me when I am dead." He then asked that the poison be brought to him. His friend, Crito, reminded him, ". . . that in other cases people have dinner and enjoy their wine, and sometimes the company of those whom they love . . . and only drink the poison quite late at night. No need to hurry; there is still plenty of time."

". . . I believe," answered Socrates, "that I should gain nothing by drinking the poison a little later—I should only make myself ridiculous in my own eyes if I clung to life and hugged it when it had no more to offer. Come, do as I say and don't make difficulties."

The poison was brought and Socrates drank it in one draught with no sign of revulsion. His friends began to cry and he reprimanded them, "Calm yourselves and be brave." When he began to feel numb he lay down and the coldness spread from his legs upward. When it reached his heart, he'd been told, he would die. He covered himself in a sheet from head to toe. Just before the end he pulled the sheet from his face and said, "Crito, we ought to offer a cock to Asclepius. See to it and don't forget." Asclepius was the god of healing. The offering was Socrates' gesture of thanks for being cured of life.

Ⴟ

Phocion of Athens, statesman and former general, had been a popular man of "high moral character" throughout his long years of public life. In his eightieth year, however, in 318 B.C., he aroused the wrath of the state and citizens of Athens for several reasons: a combination of senility, bad judgment and negligence caused him to lose Piraeus, Athens' harbor city, to the Macedonians under Antipater; he publicly betrayed an old friend; and he continued to hold his position in the unpopular aristocratic party. A kangaroo court sentenced Phocion to death for losing Piraeus. As the old man was being led away to be executed an old friend cried, "How unworthily you are suffering, Phocion." The old man replied, "All the great men of Athens have met the same end."

X

"Me a conspirator? I'm too busy kissing my wife every night." Thus **Jacques Danton** jokingly brushed aside charges of criminal conspiracy leveled at him by the Revolutionary Tribunal. In fact, Danton's whole trial was marked by historical *mots,* passionate outbursts and his fiery eloquence, yet in the end his fate was to be the same as so many during the French Revolution—in 1794 he was sentenced to be guillotined, along with fourteen co-conspirators.

As the cart that held the condemned men bounced along the thronged, cobblestoned streets of Paris, one noise rose above the weeping, pleading, praying and cursing of the occupants—that of Danton's huge, hilarious laughter. The cart passed the Café du Parnasse, the scene of Danton's first love affair. "Gabrielle," he whispered. Further on, they passed the shuttered house of Robespierre, prompting Danton to prophesy, "Robespierre, you will follow me!" Arriving at the Place de la Revolution, Danton shouted at the *lécheuses de la guillotine* (these were men and women paid by the Committee of General Security to cheer and applaud each execution, shouting, "Long live the Republic," in order to incite and excite the crowd), "Stupid clods! They'll shout 'Long live the Republic' when the Republic no longer has a head."

Because Danton was to be the last of the fifteen executed, he attempted to kiss the first, Héraut Séchelles, goodbye as Séchelles was led away. When they were thrust apart Danton reportedly turned to a guard and spat, "Fool! Do you think you can stop our heads from kissing in the basket?" Danton watched calmly as his friends were decapitated one by one, the executioners and prisoners alike slipping and sliding in the ever-growing pool of gore surrounding the guillotine.

Finally Danton himself stepped up on the scaffolding and said softly, "I shall never see you again, darling," surely thinking of his sixteen-year-old bride. Danton then turned toward the executioner, and after muttering, "Come, Danton, no weakness," ordered him to "Display my head to the crowd—it is worth it, it will be some time before they see its like again."

X

On October 16, 1793, **Marie Antoinette** rode through the streets of Paris in a style to which she was not accustomed. Her hands, instead of waving from the window of her coach drawn by six white horses, were tied tightly behind her as the cart she stood in was hauled to the guillotine.

Her hair was cut close to her scalp to insure a clean cut, and she wore a white chemise. Determined to die with dignity, Marie Antoinette spoke very little on this last ride. She cocked her head haughtily at the mostly silent, sometimes jeering throngs lining her route. When the cart stopped, the queen nearly lost control of her emotions; to stop her tears she moved very quickly. She stepped out of the cart and sped up the steps of the scaffold. She moved fast enough to trip over one of her shoes, stepping on the foot of her executioner. "I beg your pardon," she said, "I did not mean it."

X

The behavior of **Madame du Barry** at her execution has been, for many, a source of satisfaction as well as a subject for ridicule. Unlike the icy Antoinette or the scores of shocked and silent victims before and after her, Jeanne Bécu du Barry responded to her impending death in an undignified, cowardly and altogether understandable fashion. Mistress of Louis XV, illegitimate daughter of a seamstress, du Barry was a flirtatious, beautiful woman who was known for the gentleness of her nature.

One of the prosecutors for the People during the reign of terror, a M. Grième, made it his business to add du Barry to his personal list of fifteen heads. After arresting and raping the woman, Grième trumped up charge after charge in the trial that led to her condemnation. When the sentence was pronounced du Barry screamed until she fainted into the arms of the gendarmes, much to the delight of the spectators.

On the morning of her execution Madame du Barry attempted to buy her life back by divulging in detail the whereabouts of her fabulous collections of jewels. But as soon as her listeners had written down her directions she was dragged to the cart that carried its riders to their deaths. Grième said that night, "Never have I laughed so much as I did today when I saw the grimaces that beauty made when she was facing death."

It is said that during the ride Madame du Barry crouched in the corner of the cart (which she shared with four men), shuddering convulsively and crying out to the people lining the route to save her. Some of them were apparently touched and there were cries that this was murder. By the time the tumbrel stopped du Barry was hysterical and it was decided that she should be executed first. The executioner lifted her out of the cart and shoved her up the steps of the scaffold. She was being tied to the plank when she screamed, "You are going to hurt me, please don't hurt me, just one more moment, I beg you!" With a last giant effort she broke free of the

executioner and his assistants and ran to the other side of the plat-
form where she was seized immediately and returned to the plank.
She was quickly tied down, and, able to struggle no more, Madame
du Barry cried out one long howl which lasted until the blade
severed her head.

X

"The truth of it is, there is nothing in history which is so improving
to the reader, as those accounts which we meet with of the deaths
of eminent persons, and of their behavior in that dreadful season . . ." wrote the celebrated essayist and poet, **Joseph Addison.**
Addison was much interested in the manner in which men behaved
at the time of their deaths; he had closely studied the deaths of Sir
Thomas More, Petronius Arbiter, Seneca, Cato and Augustus, and
was working on a tragedy about the death of Socrates at the time of
his own. He felt a man should meet his own death with a sort of
philosophical, cheerful fortitude.

In 1719 Addison was in his late forties, married to an older woman
(unhappily, many say), asthmatic, and in the same sorry physical
shape of many overfed, heavy-drinking idle gentlemen in eighteenth-century London. By June 17 Addison was on his deathbed.
Undoubtedly he had put a great deal of thought into his own
deathbed scene; at any rate, his last scene is famous.

Addison called for his stepson, the errant Earl of Warwick. "Dear
Sir!" spoke the earl, "You sent for me, I believe, and I hope that
you have some commands. I shall hold them most sacred." Addison reached for the earl's hand. "See in what peace a Christian
can die." His moment over and message delivered, Addison died.

The scene has seemed to some pompous and theatrical. "Unluckily
he died of brandy," wrote Horace Walpole. "Nothing makes a
Christian die in peace like being maudlin." Others have defended

him. "Nor can one grudge him, his pious scene; there had been too little drama in the life of Addison," wrote James Sutherland, a biographer. Whatever one's feelings on Addison's last words, it appears the message was totally lost upon the young earl, whose extravagant living sent him to an early grave two years later.

X

Giacomo Casanova, humorist, traveler, writer and charlatan is perhaps the most well-known seducer in history. In his self-advertising and self-mocking *Memoirs* he records almost two hundred conquests. On June 4, 1798, Casanova died at the age of seventy-three. After the last sacraments were administered, he whispered loudly, "I have lived as a philosopher and am dying a Christian."

X

In 1791 religious reformer **John Wesley** was attempting to speak to those surrounding his deathbed but was too weak to make himself understood. He stopped talking and lay gathering his strength for a few minutes and then said clearly, "The best of all is, God is with us." He paused and repeated the line that has since become a byword of Methodism. He could not speak through the following night but was heard to murmur the lines of his favorite hymn, "I'll praise, I'll praise" repeatedly. At ten o'clock the next morning Wesley awoke, said to the circle of friends around him in a clear voice, "Farewell," and was gone.

X

Dr. P. J. Van Pelt tried valiantly to convert **Aaron Burr** to Christianity during the ex−vice-president's last months. His efforts, like those of other well-meaning clergymen, came to nought. The notorious and brilliant Burr would not be intimidated by his approaching death. In September of 1836 it became apparent that Burr's time was running out and Van Pelt increased his efforts. On September 13 Burr's doctors agreed that this was probably his last day on earth. Through the night Van Pelt stayed with Burr and on the following morning asked him if he was ready to accept salvation. Burr said, "On that subject I am coy." He fell asleep moments later and died that afternoon.

X

Solomon Foot, senator from Vermont, died in March 1866 after a month-long illness. During that month he was visited by many of his colleagues from Congress. All left his bedside moved and impressed by the faith and peace which the senator displayed. At seven in the morning on March 28 Foot asked to be lifted up to see the sun shining on the dome of the Capitol, but his sight was so dim by this time that he could not make it out. Soon after he held his wife in his arms and said, as breathing became difficult, "What, can this be death? So easy? Is it come already?" Minutes later, his eyes wide open, he lifted up his arms and said, "I see it! I see it! The gates are wide open! Beautiful!" Without a shudder he died immediately.

X

Thomas Paine never complained about the intensity of his suffering during his last months, though the pain became so great at times he would, in the final weeks, cry out involuntarily, "Oh, Lord help me." His mind stayed unclouded and he retained his sense of humor. When his doctor, referring to Paine's distended abdomen, said, "Your belly diminishes," Paine replied, "And yours augments."

In *The Age of Reason* Paine refuted the divinity of Jesus Christ, saying of the four gospels, "It is, I believe, impossible to find so many and such glaring absurdities, contradictions and falsehoods as are in these books." During a visit to Paine on one of his last days, Dr. James Manly hopefully asked him, "Do you believe—or let me qualify the question—do you wish to believe that Jesus Christ is the son of God?" After a long silence Paine said with passion, "I have no wish to believe on that subject." He died quietly soon after on the morning of June 8, 1809.

⊠

Fyodor Dostoevsky, when looking for spiritual guidance in times of crisis, would open his Bible, turn to the New Testament and read the first lines his gaze fell upon. They always seemed appropriate and Dostoevsky the gambler had faith in the significance of his random choices.

On Sunday, January 25, 1881, Dostoevsky suffered a sudden hemorrhage. The doctor was summoned and, after examining the patient, assured the family that the situation was not too serious. But for the next few days Dostoevsky weakened steadily. On the morning of January 28 he asked his wife to open the Bible and read to him the first words she saw. She read aloud, ". . . And Jesus answering said unto him: Hold me not back for thus it becometh us to fulfill all righteousness." Dostoevsky said, "Did you hear? Hold me not back. My hour has come. I must die." After bidding farewell to his wife and children he slowly lost consciousness and died that evening.

⊠

Several widely varied versions of the murder of **Grigori Rasputin,** "The Mad Monk," have been reported, and the details of what actually occurred on December 16 and 17, 1916, may never be known. But one thing is certain: Rasputin was a very difficult man to kill. The generally accepted story was provided by Prince Feliks Yusupov, the architect of the homicide and one of its chief perpetrators. The story as told by Maria Rasputin (Grigori's daughter) and Patte Barham, co-biographers of Rasputin, is even bloodier and more depraved than Yusupov's. Patte Barham wrote: "[Our] account of Rasputin's murder has been reconstructed from two sources: the partly fictitious narrative of his principal murderer, Prince Feliks Felikovich Yusupov, and the story told by one of the Prince's servants to his [the servant's] sister-in-law, and by her related to me."

Yusupov's version is essentially the one that follows. The twice removed servant—sister-in-law additions and divergences are inserted in parentheses. Pick your favorite.

The state of the Russian monarchy in the year 1916 was, as most people know, somewhat less than stable. Among the many accusations and rumors flying about in this unsettled time was the theory that the Tsar and Tsarina (especially the latter) were under the evil control of Grigori Rasputin, the religious leader and charismatic healer whom some believed to be the devil incarnate. Prince Feliks Yusupov was a friend of Rasputin who apparently became convinced by a political activist, V. M. Purishkevich, that Rasputin was, in fact, undermining the Russian monarchy through his bad influence on the Tsarina. Yusupov and Purishkevich decided to kill the holy man. (Another motive, the chief one according to Maria Rasputin, was Yusupov's hatred of Rasputin for spurning the young Prince's sexual advances.) They enlisted three other men to help: Captain Ivan Sukhotin, an officer; Grand Duke Dmitri Pavlovich, friend to Yusupov; and Dr. Stanislas Lazovert, who prepared the poison.

On the night of December 16, 1916, in St. Petersburg, Prince Yusupov invited Rasputin to his palace to meet his wife. Members of the Rasputin household, wary of a plot, urged him not to go. Pooh-poohing their fears, he left as scheduled at 12:15 A.M. when the Prince picked him up. At the palace Prince Feliks led Rasputin to a basement room and explained there was a party going on upstairs and that his wife would be down as soon as the guests departed. The Prince offered cyanide-laced port to Rasputin, which Grigori accepted, and also proffered similarly flavored cakes and candies to his guest. Rasputin ate and drank freely of the poisoned repast. (Maria Rasputin said her father never ate sweets, though he was very partial to wine.)

To Yusupov's amazement the poison had no discernible effect on the holy man. In fact, he seemed content and happy and even asked the Prince to sing and play a few tunes to while away the time. After the entertainment, Yusupov excused himself and went upstairs to confer with his confederates. The flustered Yusupov explained to his friends that the poison was not working. Strangling was discussed as an option. Finally it was decided that they would shoot him.

Revolver in pocket, Yusupov went back downstairs to find Rasputin admiring a crystal cross. Yusupov said, "Grigori, you had better say a prayer before it." Seeming to understand his predicament, Rasputin turned to the cross, and at this moment Prince Feliks Yusupov shot him in the back. (It is at the point of Yusupov's entry that the Rasputin-Barham account alters radically from the Prince's. According to them, all the murderers entered the room behind Yusupov, threw Rasputin to the floor and proceeded to gang-rape him. Rasputin reportedly said to them, "May God forgive you." After the rape Yusupov fired one shot into Rasputin's head. Rasputin then murmured, "What do you want of me?" and, as if on cue, the group again attacked the raped, bullet-pierced, poison-filled body, kicking and punching him repeatedly. The attack culminated in the castration of Rasputin.)

Yusupov's men entered the room after the shot and the doctor pronounced him dead. Two of them took Rasputin's coat, one of them put it on, and they drove from the palace to make it appear that Rasputin departed alive and well. Yusupov and Purishkevich went upstairs. (M. R. and P. B. say they remained downstairs.) About an hour later, Yusupov returned to the basement and, while looking over the body, thought he detected an eyelid quivering. (From here on the two versions are in accord.) To assure himself that Rasputin was indeed dead, Yusupov shook the body violently. Suddenly Rasputin rose up and grasped the Prince's shoulders fiercely, tearing off an epaulet. Horrified, Yusupov tore himself out of the iron grip and fled up the stairs.

While Yusupov was rather breathlessly explaining that Rasputin was far from dead, the indefatigable mad monk was crawling across the floor and up the stairs until he came to a locked door which led to the courtyard. He burst through the door and began to stagger across the snow toward the palace gates. On hearing the noise Yusupov and Purishkevich ran out and fired four shots, hitting Rasputin twice, in the shoulder and the head. Rasputin fell. The two men turned on the bloody, still body, raining kicks and blows. At this point the others returned with the car. Rasputin's hands were tied behind his back and he was driven to the nearest river and thrown through a hole in the ice.

The body was discovered a few days later. According to the autopsy report (there is no mention of castration and rape; though it is possible this type of evidence might have been withheld) Rasputin did not die as a result of the poison he had ingested, nor the beatings and knifing he suffered, nor the three bullets in his head and body. His left hand had escaped from its bonds, his wrists were scarred and his lungs were filled with water. Rasputin had drowned.

Filial devotion among the members of royalty in ancient Rome was often not what it was cracked up to be. The young Emperor Nero, who succeeded Claudius after **Agrippina,** Nero's mother, poisoned the old man, decided in A.D. 59 that his mother's attempts on his own life were becoming annoying. He devised an elaborate plan to have Agrippina killed on a boat taking her home from one of his parties. The first part of the plot failed when Agrippina escaped and swam to shore. Agrippina was in her room at home when the captain of the ship and two of his officers walked in to finish the job they had bungled on the sea. On entering, one of the men struck the emperor's mother with a club and they all drew their swords. Agrippina pulled off her nightgown and cried out to the murderers, "Strike me in the womb." It took a full five minutes to kill her.

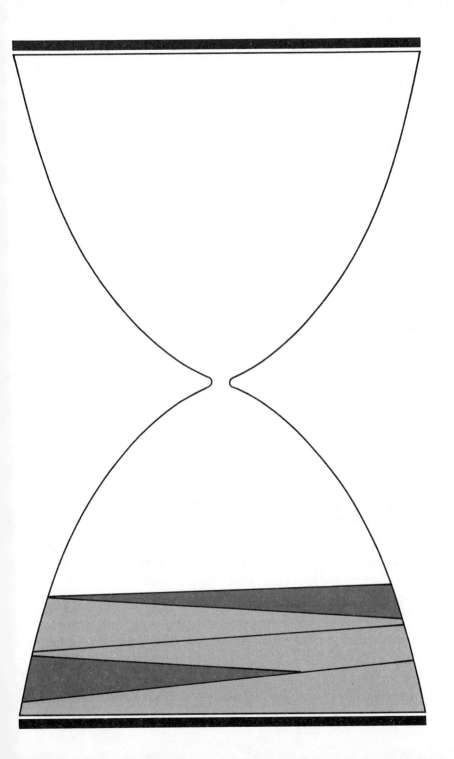

King **Henry IV** of France was an exception. The man who united France after the vicious, divisive religious wars, Henry was one of the only truly civilized, tolerant and humane monarchs of his (or any other) day. On the night of May 14, 1610, the king got into his coach to visit his friend and counselor, the Duke of Rosny. The coach was halted for a moment on the Rue de la Ferronérie to wait for a couple of carts to go by. At that moment François Ravaillac, a deranged religious zealot, leapt onto a wheel of the coach and stabbed Henry. "I am wounded!" cried the king. When Ravaillac stabbed him a second time, penetrating his heart, Henry sighed loudly, said "It's nothing," and died.

$$\rm X$$

On the evening of April 3, 1968, **Martin Luther King, Jr.,** spoke to a crowd of 2,000 people in Memphis, Tennessee. Part of his speech went as follows: "And then I got to Memphis. And some began to . . . talk about threats that were out. Or what would happen to me from some of our sick white brothers. . . . But it really doesn't matter with me now. Because I've been to the mountain top. I won't mind. Like anybody I would like to live a long life. . . . But I'm not concerned about that now. . . . I've seen the promised land. I may not get there with you, but I want you to know that we as the people will get to the promised land. So I'm happy tonight. . . . I'm not fearing any man. Mine eyes have seen the glory of the coming of the Lord."

The next evening King stepped out of his second-floor hotel room onto the balcony and exchanged some words with Reverend Jesse Jackson in the courtyard below. Jackson introduced King to Ben Branch, a musician who was to perform later in the evening at a rally. King said to him, "Be sure and sing 'Precious Lord Take My Hand,' " adding, "Sing it real pretty." At that moment the shot was fired. King died on the way to the hospital.

Frederick Douglass was born into slavery in 1817. At the age of twenty-one he escaped and made his way north. In 1841, in New Bedford, Massachusetts, Douglass gave his first speech, beginning a lifetime of speaking and fighting for the rights of black men and women. In his later years Douglass enjoyed unusually good health. When talking about death he often said he would like "to fall as the leaf in the autumn of life."

On February 2, 1895, Douglass dined with his wife. After the meal he prepared to go to a nearby church where he was to give a speech. On his way out of the dining room he fell to his knees, so slowly and calmly that his wife was not alarmed. With a surprised look Douglass said, "Why, what does this mean?" and stretched out on the floor, dying immediately.

X

Robert Louis Stevenson spent the morning of December 3, 1894, dictating the ninth chapter of *Weir of Hermiston* to his step-daughter, Bell Strong. He was in high spirits as he rattled on to Belle about future chapters and his own past. In the afternoon, after writing a few letters, Stevenson went downstairs and attempted to cheer up his wife Fanny, playing cards with her, chatting about future plans, teasing and joking. Fanny was depressed, struck with one of her powerful feelings of foreboding, something Stevenson attempted to minimize without mocking. Stevenson suggested bringing up a particularly good bottle of Burgundy for dinner, and offered to make his special mayonnaise for the salad.

He was "gaily talking," flushed with creative afterglow, when after strolling onto the veranda he suddenly clasped his hands to his head and exclaimed, "What's that?" and then quickly to Fanny, "Do I look strange?" After collapsing to his knees, unconscious, he was helped onto a big easy chair. Stevenson had suffered a cerebral hemorrhage. He never regained consciousness, and died at ten past eight that evening, at the age of forty-four.

X

On December 16, 1928, **Elinor Wylie** sat reading in her Ninth Street apartment in New York City. She had spent her day arranging and rearranging the order of some poems that were to be sent off to the printers the following morning. The order settled upon, Wylie was enjoying a quiet Sunday evening. She asked her husband for a glass of water. As he handed it to her, she asked, "Is that all it is?" and fell back into her chair, dead. She was forty-three years old.

X

Sunday, February 14, 1938, found the newspaper columnist **Oscar Odd McIntyre** writing notes for his Monday evening column. Syndicated by more than 500 daily and Sunday papers around the country, McIntyre wrote about New York with the wide-eyed wonder of a country visitor and had done so throughout his career. A Christian Scientist and recluse, a long-ill anemic who always thought he was sicker than he was, McIntyre forbade any discussion of his health in his home. The last word he wrote was "success," before setting his pen aside.

Maybelle, his wife of thirty years, entered the bedroom, saying to him, "And now, if you don't mind, I'm going to take a little snooze for myself," and lay down on the bed beside him. Both their anniversary and McIntyre's birthday were four days away. McIntyre called to her, "Snooks, will you please turn this way? I like to look at your face." Smiling, she did so. McIntyre gazed upon her for a long while, then closed his eyes for the last time. He died at midnight.

X

The Irish political leader **Charles Parnell** was an extremely superstitious man. One of his beliefs was that if there came a time when he was unable to sleep for two consecutive nights it would be a signal of his impending death. Parnell had not been well, and on Sunday, October 4, 1891, he did not sleep. The next day he became increasingly feverish. He and his bride of three months, Katharine, chatted about their future together when "We will be so happy, Queenie, there are so many things happier than politics."

Parnell did not sleep on Monday night either, dozing intermittently on Tuesday, his fever raging. Katharine heard him say, "the Conservative party" once, but he was mostly quiet, responding to her caresses with smiles. Late Tuesday evening Parnell woke abruptly and said to Katharine, "Kiss me, sweet Wifie, and I will try to sleep a little." She lay beside him on the bed as they shared a long kiss, shortly after which Parnell fell unconscious. He was never to regain consciousness, dying shortly before midnight.

X

The Restoration comic dramatist and poet **William Wycherley** was in his mid-seventies when his young cousin, Captain Thomas Shrimpton, came to him with a proposition. Shrimpton knew Wycherley badly needed money with which to pay off his debts, and also knew Wycherley could not get at his own inheritance.

Wycherley's father's estate, in the hands of Wycherley's nephew, had a handsome provision for any widow the old man might leave (app. £400 per annum). Shrimpton suggested that Wycherley marry a young woman of Shrimpton's acquaintance, the possessor of a large (said to be £1500) cash dowry. It seems Wycherley, who was ill, was interested in injuring his nephew anyway, and had at one time told the young Alexander Pope that he would marry as soon as his life was despaired of.

Shrimpton was persuasive; spurred on by drink and perhaps by threats of debtors' prison Wycherley and the young woman were married. His young bride was a shameless fortune hunter, and, not coincidentally, she was Shrimpton's mistress. Eleven days after the marriage in 1716 an ailing Wycherley called his young bride to his bedside and begged her not to deny him one last request. After she promised she would not, he said, "My dear, it is only this, that you will never marry an old man again." It was the last request he would make. About this wonderful sarcasm Pope commented, "I think his request a little hard, for why should he bar her from doubling her jointure in the same easy terms." Wycherley's newly wealthly widow granted him his last request. Shortly after his death she married Shrimpton.

X

Oliver Goldsmith, critic, poet and dramatist, whose appetite for food and fine clothing nearly matched his inability to pay for either, lay dying of a kidney ailment. The attendant physician, Dr. Turton, took Goldsmith's pulse and said, "Your pulse is in greater disorder than it should be from the state of fever which you have. Is your mind at ease?" Goldsmith's reply was brief. "No, it is not." This was his last sentence. He fell asleep, and after waking briefly, in convulsions, at 4:00 A.M., died at 4:30 A.M., April 3, 1774.

Julius Beerbohm, half-brother to writer Max Beerbohm, was a dandy. Indeed, his overriding concern for appearances remained with him to the last moments of his life. In 1956 when his brother Herbert visited Julius at his deathbed, he was wearing a ginger-colored suit which Julius simply could not tolerate. He looked at Herbert, said with extreme distaste, "Ginger!" and turned, facing the wall, refusing to speak to his brother any further. He died soon afterward.

X

William Gilbert of Gilbert and Sullivan (he wrote the words) expressed his feelings about the medical profession when he asked a friend what her boy was going to be when he grew up. "He's going into medicine," was the reply. "Hm," said Gilbert, "I don't mind his going into medicine as long as his medicine doesn't go into me." And, in fact, the aging Gilbert's own diet of fish and fresh fruits and vegetables succeeded in improving his health more than all the doctors' previous advice.

In his later years, which were his healthiest and happiest ones, Gilbert surrounded himself with beautiful women. There was a room in his home which he titled "The Flirtorium" and, by all accounts, flirting was enough for Gilbert in his late sixties and early seventies. And he was good at it. He told one woman, "I am rapidly relapsing into a condition of babbling dotage. I am a crumbling ruin—a magnificent ruin, no doubt, but still a ruin—and, like all ruins, I look best by moonlight."

On May 29, 1911, the seventy-four-year-old dramatist had a date with two young women to go swimming in his lake. Before the rendezvous he lunched at his club in London. When he joined the actor W. H. Kendall at his table Kendall was understandably astonished, as the two had not spoken for many years as a result of old, almost forgotten quarrels. Gilbert was charming at lunch, reminiscing warmly with his old enemy. He shook hands goodbye with Kendall three separate times before he left, saying, "I must be off, as I've an appointment to teach a young lady to swim."

It was a warm day and the two girls changed into bathing suits more quickly than Gilbert. They were already in the lake when he appeared at its edge. One of the two realized at that moment that she was in over her head and became frightened, calling out to her friend for help. Gilbert yelled out, "It's not very deep, don't splash, you'll be all right," and dove in. When he reached her he said, "Put your hands on my shoulders and don't struggle." When she followed his instructions, Gilbert sank beneath her. The girl found her footing and made it to shore but Gilbert did not. He had suffered a fatal heart attack.

X

On May 25, 1895, **Oscar Wilde,** who a few months earlier was the brightest star in the firmament of literary London's high society, was sentenced to two years of hard labor in a British prison for making love to men. A few months later, in Reading Gaol, suffering from an almost complete physical and mental breakdown, Wilde rose one morning to begin his day of work. In his weakened state the buttoning of his shirt proved too much for him and he fell over, landing on the stone floor on the side of his head. Five years later (and three years out of prison) he died from complications resulting from a middle ear injury sustained on that occasion.

Toward the end of September 1900, Wilde (now living in Paris in voluntary exile) was struck by a recurrence of the ear trouble he had suffered in prison and was confined to bed. On October 10 he was operated on. The precise nature of the operation is unknown, but it was not successful and may, indeed, have hastened his decline.

Reggie Turner and Robert Ross, his closest friends, visited often during the weeks following the operation. Wilde was described by Ross as being in ". . . very good spirits and though he assured me his sufferings were dreadful, at the same time he shouted with laughter and told many stories against the doctors and himself." It was on one of these visits that Wilde, sipping on a glass of iced champagne, remarked, "I am dying as I've lived: beyond my means."

Wilde was able to go out two or three times during the end of October. On these occasions he went to a cafe in the Latin Quarter where he insisted on drinking absinthe. When Reggie Turner reprimanded him about his self-destructive consumption of alcohol Wilde replied in a mock-congratulatory tone, "You are qualifying for a doctor. When you can refuse bread to the hungry, and drink to the thirsty, you may apply for your Diploma."

As a result of these excursions Wilde developed a cold, which aggravated his ear condition. He was again confined to his quarters where he was intermittently severely despondent and almost manically joyful. One day, very depressed, he said to Ross and Turner that he had dreamed the night before that he was "supping with the dead." "My dear Oscar," said Turner, "you must have been the life and soul of the party." This response delighted Oscar who, according to Ross, then "became high-spirited again, almost hysterical."

During the early part of November Wilde's doctors were confident he would recover. But soon afterward he contracted cerebral meningitis and on November 30, after being baptized into the Catholic Church, Oscar Wilde died.

X

On December 10th, 1896, the city of Paris was outraged, shocked and delighted by **Alfred Jarry**'s play, *Ubu Roi.* ·The first word of the play, *"Merdre"* (a play on the French word "merde" which means "shit"—variously translated as "shittre" or "pshitt"), created a pandemonium in the crowded theater that lasted fifteen minutes. Many walked out; the rest of the audience separated vocally into two hysterical factions, some of whom came to blows. The second word of the play, *"merdre"* caused a similar reaction, and the audience continued to interrupt the now legendary, monstrous farce many times during the evening. The scatalogical classic played that one night and not again until 1908, a year after Jarry's death.

Jarry, only twenty-three in 1896, became an instant celebrity. He also became so obsessed with, and committed to, the character of Père Ubu that he virtually transformed himself into his king of Pataphysics (Jarry's own science) based on a sort of anti-reason. In the world of Père Ubu everything is turned upside-down. So Jarry began all his meals with dessert and ended with the appetizers. He adopted the character's gestures and nasal tone. The language he began using (employing the royal "we" and substituting nouns with descriptive phrases such as, for a bicycle: "that which rolls"; for a bird: "that which chirps") is still heard in certain literary circles in Paris.

Alfred Jarry died of tuberculosis at the age of thirty-four. He would have lived much longer had he not taken murderous portions of absinthe and ether all his life. Consistent with his character, Jarry was not merely unashamed of his constant, intense, almost hallucinatory drunkenness, he called alcohol his "holy water" and "the essence of life."

As Jarry's body and mind continued to be destroyed, he became too ill to leave his lodgings as often as he was used to, and after a conspicuously long absence some friends became worried and dropped by his home. After knocking on the door for some time they heard Jarry's voice, weak and strained, saying he was coming. They waited; he didn't come. They knocked again and asked if they should call for a locksmith. Jarry replied, "It might not be such a bad idea after all." When they entered Jarry's room his friends found him lying on his bed, paralyzed from the waist down, close to death.

In the hospital Jarry was visited, in his few lucid moments, by friends, one of whom became so upset he turned from the bed to cry. Jarry said, "Well, Polti, aren't you feeling well today?"

During the last few days of his life Jarry muttered over and over, *"Je cherche . . . je cherche . . . je cherche,"* ("I look for"), but never finished the sentence. At the very end Jarry made a last request. He wanted a toothpick. When it was given to him, writes Dr. Saltas, "It seemed as if he were suddenly filled with a great joy. . . . I barely stepped aside to speak to the nurse when she signalled me to turn around. He was drawing his last breath."

X

Ernest Dowson, the poet who wrote the beautiful love poem *"Non sum qualis eram bonae sub regno Cynarae,"* spent his last weeks destitute and desperately ill in the home of his friends, the Robert Sherards. Though none too prosperous themselves, and able to offer Dowson only a small room, a cot, and the barest of necessities, the Sherards provided Dawson a refuge, and freedom from rent worries. A combination of tuberculosis, too much absinthe and sheer nervous exhaustion had reduced Dowson to a skeleton; he rarely stirred from his room, amusing himself instead with the company of

Mrs. Sherard, her little son and his reading. He talked frequently of traveling to the south of France, or Italy, and of the dinners and presents he would buy the Sherards "when my ship comes in."

On the morning of February 23, 1900, Dowson was seized with one of the coughing attacks that plagued him, prompting him to send to the chemist for some ipecacuanna wine. Dowson was distrustful of doctors, and would not consent to see one, preferring patent medicines. Usually the Sherards humored him, but in this instance Robert Sherard realized a doctor was crucial, and went to send for one, leaving Dowson in the care of Mrs. Sherard. As she held the dying man in her arms he said to her, "You are like an angel from heaven—God bless you." Minutes later, Robert Sherard returned to the room and said, "You had better get up, Ernest, and sit in the armchair. You will breathe more easily." Sherard tried to raise him, but Dowson's body was limp. He was only thirty-three years old.

X

Edgar Allan Poe boarded a steamer in Richmond, Virginia, bound for Baltimore City on September 27, 1849. In Baltimore on October 3, a friend of Poe's, Dr. J. E. Snodgrass, received the following note from a stranger. "Dear Sir: There is a gentleman, rather the worse for wear, at Ryan's 4th ward polls, who goes under the cognomen of Edgar A. Poe, and who appears in great distress, and says he is acquainted with you, and I assure you, he is in need of immediate assistance. Yours in haste, Jos. W. Walker."

America's first great man of letters certainly was. Wearing tattered, ill-fitting clothing, Poe was lying in an apparent drunken stupor in a gutter outside a saloon when Walker, a printer for the *Baltimore Sun,* discovered him. He took notice of Poe because of a fine malacca cane Poe was holding. After carrying Poe into the barroom

Walker sent his note, and by 5 P.M. Poe was a patient in the Washington College Hospital. His doctors, both active in the temperance movement, at first irritated by having to treat someone they thought was merely another drunk, soon realized the gravity of Poe's condition (both diabetes and a brain tumor have been suggested by biographers). Poe's drinking and subsequent "alcoholism" have been greatly misunderstood; rather than being a heavy drinker, Poe suffered a great intolerance for alcohol—so much so that as little as one drink could have a violent, adverse effect upon him. This combined with the facts that he could be a particularly nasty drunk and tended to be a binge drinker gave rise to Poe's hard-drinking reputation.

Poe was mostly delirious during his last days, and apart from telling the doctors he had a wife in Richmond, virtually no information was ever gleaned about the five days between Richmond and Baltimore City. They remain a mystery to this day. The following three days were grim, with Poe crying out and moaning in his delirium, which was becoming more violent. He talked constantly, engaging in "vacant converse with spectral and imaginary objects on the walls." Saturday night he began calling for "Reynolds! Oh Reynolds."

Jeremiah Reynolds was the author of *Mocha Dick, or the White Whale of the Pacific* and other sea-going stories that Poe had loved as a younger man. Poe's *Arthur Gordon Pym* was inspired by a projected South Seas expedition of Reynolds. Now these tales seemed to be haunting him. The halls of the hospital resounded with Reynolds's name through Saturday night and into Sunday morning. By 3:00 A.M. on October 7, Poe was resting quietly, apparently exhausted by his exertions. Moving his head to one side he whispered his last words, "Lord help my poor soul."

X

In 1928 at the age of fifty-eight, having survived her beloved sister and her mother, and with two siblings in asylums, **Charlotte Mew**, an English poet, drank a bottle of disinfectant and died. When doctors attempted to revive the writer of the lines

Smile, Death, see I smile as I come to you. . . .
. . . (Show me your face, why the eyes are kind!)

she said to them in her last conscious moment, "Don't keep me. Let me go."

X

Returning home on November 29, 1931, after a series of poetry readings, the poet **Vachel Lindsay** shared a quiet evening with his wife Elizabeth (which she later remembered as "very sweet"). The next morning Lindsay demanded of her, "Who was that man you met downstairs last night? Was it your father coming to blackmail me, or somebody else, or a group of people? You can't fool me, I heard you all talking. What's more, you came upstairs and dressed and painted your face, and brushed your hair three separate times. And you said, as you went out, 'Don't tell any of them that you are my husband. If you do, they will kill you.'"

This sort of accusation had become more frequent as Lindsay grew more insane. A combination of his pressing debts, his declining poetical reputation, the increasingly difficult time he had in writing, the age difference between he and the younger Elizabeth (twenty-one years) and an undiagnosed disease—perhaps idiopathic epilepsy—all contributed to his mental confusion. During the next few days Lindsay would at one moment be playing with his children, or resting, and at the next suffering violent outbursts; first raving at his father-in-law (whom he was convinced was conspiring to murder him), then imploring his wife always to remember that he loved her.

December 4 found Lindsay joking and talking at a tea party while Elizabeth was secretly consulting with doctors. Upon her return home the last awful evening began. It started with Lindsay weeping inconsolably. Later, he whipped himself into a tremendous rage, ranting about every insult real or imagined from boyhood on, stopping to dwell upon the night Elizabeth robbed him of his virginity, then moving on to their married life, all the while punctuating his tirade with protestations of his great love for her. He pendulated between extremes, talking about her father's "murder plot" and threatening to leave. Finally he went to bed, where, finding him quietly reading, she joined him.

After a while Lindsay stormed downstairs. Elizabeth followed. Lindsay appeared to her to be much more "calm, happy, peaceful, and firm." She asked him if he was all right. "Yes, dear, I'm quite all right. I'll be up in a little while." Fifteen minutes later Elizabeth, now asleep, awoke to the sounds of a terrific commotion. Lindsay was running around furiously downstairs. He crashed up the stairs toward the hall. Elizabeth thought Lindsay's mind had finally snapped, and that he was en route to murder their children and herself. Running out to stop him, she screamed. His face was maniacal, eyes bulging, hands waving. She embraced him, put him into their bed, gave him some water and begged him to tell her what was wrong.

"I just tried to kill myself by drinking Lysol," he said. As Elizabeth ran to call the doctor, Lindsay hurled the water across the room, and shaking his fists, shouted, "I got them before they could get me—they can just try to explain this, if they can!" They were his last words. Elizabeth and the maid tried every antidote listed on the Lysol label, but Lindsay died minutes after the doctor's arrival. His death was reported to the world at large as heart failure.

Ⅹ

The poet and essayist **Alice Meynell** was known for the exactness, simplicity and thoughtfulness of her writing. She ranks with the great poets of the late nineteenth century, and was certainly among the most prolific. Her last months were occupied in preparing an anthology of poetry for children and her *Last Poems* (1923), both of which were to be published posthumously. Once bedridden she desired privacy; she was painfully aware of the cruelties old age sometimes wreaks upon one's personal appearance, so much so that she preferred her children not visit her. Meynell wanted them to remember her as she had been. Her daughter Viola tells that when Meynell's son Francis last visited her she turned away from him, offered her hand and said, "He shall have my bluest veins to kiss!" The end of her life came on November 27, 1922. She died in her sleep, her last recorded words being, "This is not tragic. I am happy."

X

Catholic convert, English Jesuit and poet **Gerard Manley Hopkins** died at the age of forty-four while his parents stood by his bedside. Father Wheeler, Hopkins's friend (and his nurse during the last days) administered the sacrament of Extreme Unction to the poet on June 6, 1889. A typhoid victim, Hopkins could barely speak to answer the prayers spoken by Father Wheeler. He was able, with great effort, to whisper the words, "I am so happy. I am so happy," just before he died.

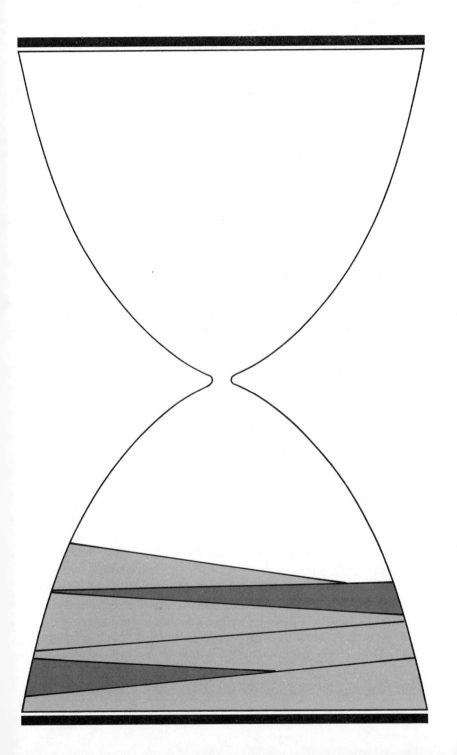

Having caught a severe chill in the winter of 1814, Prince **Charles de Ligne** lay dying in Vienna with his wife, daughters and some friends gathered about his bed. The old soldier, diplomatist, traveler and writer (a great favorite of both Maria Theresa and Catherine II of Russia, friend to Frederick the Great, Voltaire, Rousseau) was softly speaking to his loved ones: "I always admired the end of Petronius, who died to the sound of music and good poetry. Well, I am more fortunate. I die surrounded by my friends, and in the arms of those I love. I may not be strong enough to live longer, but I am strong enough to love you."

He was delirious at times, but when his daughters knelt by his bedside praying, he was sharp enough to chastise them tenderly: "What are you doing, children? Do you take me for a relic? Wait a little; I am not yet a saint." Alternately high-spirited and feverish, at midnight de Ligne rose up and ordered, "Advance! Long live Maria Theresa!" These were his last recorded words.

☒

Maria Theresa, religious zealot, Empress of Austria and mother of Marie Antoinette (and fifteen other children), died of complications resulting from a severe chill on November 29, 1780. The Empress would take no sedatives during her last days, and on the evening of her death she explained why: "You want me to sleep?" she said. "While at any moment I shall be called before my Judge, I am afraid to ·sleep. I must not be taken unawares. I wish to see death coming." A few hours later, unable to breathe, she hoisted herself up from her chair and made her way to the sofa. Her son Joseph, his arm around her, said, "Your Majesty cannot be very comfortable like that." "No," she said, "but comfortable enough to die." A minute later she did.

☒

"I look upon death," wrote **Benjamin Franklin** to a friend, "to be as necessary to our constitution as sleep. We shall rise refreshed in the morning."

Franklin lived to be eighty-four. Except for his last two years he enjoyed excellent health during his wonderfully productive life. He left the world willingly and peacefully, though in great pain. At his bedside Franklin's daughter expressed the wish that he would regain his health and live many years longer. "I hope not," said Franklin. Sometime later on that day, April 17, 1790, Franklin was advised to change his position on the bed in order to breathe more easily. He replied, "A dying man can do nothing easy." They were his last words.

⏳

July 4, 1826, the fiftieth anniversary of the signing of the Declaration of Independence, was occasion for a rather remarkable coincidence. On that day the author of the Declaration (and third president of the United States) and its staunchest defender (and second president of the United States) died. A New York newspaper said that the "like had never happened in the world, nor can it ever happen again, we may almost say with certainty." Washington, D.C.'s journal, the *National Intelligencer,* said, "No language can exaggerate it—no reason account for it. It is one of those events which have no example on record, and as a beauteous moral must forever stand alone on the page of history."

In their later years the two bitter political and philosophical rivals, **Thomas Jefferson** and **John Adams,** had corresponded frequently. A strong (albeit long-distance) friendship developed and their old debates continued with warmth rather than heat. In 1824 when Adams's son, John Quincy, was elected president, Jefferson wrote the elder Adams a letter of congratulations that concluded

79

with, "Nights of rest to you and days of tranquility are the wishes I tender you." Adams replied, "Every line from you exhilarates my spirits and gives me a glow of pleasure."

Adams's last days were sad ones. If he was thrilled about his son's achievements, he also mourned the fact that his wife Abigail (who died in 1818) could not share his joy. By April of 1826 it was clear that Adams did not have long to live. He weakened steadily during the spring and as July drew near he began to sink rapidly. At dawn July 4, Adams woke for a moment and a servant by his bedside asked, "Do you know, sir, what day it is?" "Oh yes," he replied, "it is the glorious Fourth of July. God bless it. God bless you all." He then sank into a coma and slept through the morning. He woke again at about 1:00 P.M. and spoke his last sentence, "Thomas Jefferson survives." A few hours later, just before sunset, Adams was dead.

Jefferson's health, too, steadily declined during the spring of 1826, though he was able to take short horseback rides until mid-June. Well aware that death was at hand, Jefferson only wanted to survive until July 4. But on July 3 it didn't look like he would. Jefferson dozed, his pulse barely perceptible, through July 3, speaking only once or twice. At eleven o'clock that evening, N. P. Trist, husband to one of Jefferson's granddaughters, was sitting by the bed when Jefferson asked, "This is the Fourth?" Trist did not answer. The question was repeated and Trist nodded yes, a forgivable white lie. Jefferson did actually make it through that night and into the next day. In the early afternoon of July 4, 1826, either a few minutes before John Adams was affirming Jefferson's existence or a few minutes after, Thomas Jefferson died.

On the morning of Saturday, October 23, 1852, **Daniel Webster** said to the physician at his bedside, "Doctor, you have carried me through the night, I think you will get me through today. I shall die tonight." The doctor answered, "You are right, sir."

Webster's last day was spent praying with his family and wishing them, and his servants, farewell. At one point, Mrs. Webster lost control of herself and, crying almost hysterically, wrapped her arms around her husband's neck. "My dear wife," he said gently, "when you and I were married at the Bowling Green, we knew that we must one day part."

Toward evening Webster directed all his energies to staying awake, not in an attempt to halt his approaching death, but because he wanted to be fully conscious when the moment came. He dozed off a number of times, waking suddenly and saying, "Am I alive, or am I dead?" A little after midnight he awoke and looked about, unsure of which world he was in. After making a concentrated effort to see and identify his surroundings he said, "I still live!" They were his last words; he died three hours later.

X

Henry Adams, historian, educator and grandson of John Quincy Adams, feared senility more than death. Letters from his aging peers frightened him with their repetitive and continual reminiscences of lost youth. He ordered his secretary-companion Aileen Tone to interrupt him immediately if he proved guilty of similar wanderings. Adams lived to the age of eighty, witnessing the deaths of most of his contemporaries. He occasionally saw the funeral corteges passing his house on the way to St. John's Episcopal Church. More than once he was heard to chuckle and say, "There goes another."

Adams suffered a stroke in 1912 and died six years later, his mind still functioning and his interest in world affairs unabated. On the day before his death he said, in reference to a German cannon known as Big Bertha, which was then shelling the city of Paris from seventy-six miles away, "Life is intolerable. . . . This is no world for an old man to live in when the Germans can shoot to the moon." Later on that same day he spoke his last recorded words to Miss Tone, saying passionately, "Dear child, keep me alive." The next morning she found that he had died overnight.

✕

On December 4, 1679, philosopher **Thomas Hobbes** died at the age of ninety-one "rather for want of the fuel of life than by the power of his disease," according to his executor James Wheldon. It is reported that Hobbes, upon learning he was to die, said, "I shall be glad to find a hole to creep out of the world at."

✕

The street outside **Woodrow Wilson**'s home was filled with people praying for the ex-president when he died on February 3, 1924. His health was considered improved and for the first time recovery was hoped for. But on this day Wilson knew the time had come. He whispered to his wife at his bedside, "I am ready," and died almost immediately.

✕

On the night before her death in 1963 **Edith Piaf,** one of the most adored singers of all time, reminisced with her sister. For hours she and Simone re-lived their life, together and apart. When Simone got up to leave Piaf took her hand and said, "I can die now; I've lived twice." The following morning Simone was informed by messenger that her sister was dead.

X

William Lloyd Garrison was the most vocal and most famous of abolitionist leaders. He was the founder and editor of *The Liberator,* the anti-slavery journal that helped change the course of American history.

Garrison fell ill in May 1879 and took to bed saying, "I feel as if the machinery were giving way." By May 20 his condition was grave enough for his children to remain constantly by his bedside. He became intermittently delirious and, like many, expressed repeatedly the wish to "go home." On the morning of May 23 Garrison's doctor asked if he wanted anything, to which Garrison vehemently replied, "To finish it up!" He did not speak again. He fell into a coma that evening which lasted twenty-four hours until his death.

X

Oliver Cromwell spoke a great deal to himself and his maker as he lay dying in 1658. He was heard saying at one point, "It is a fearful thing to fall into the hands of the living God." This he repeated three times. Later, when offered something to drink and advised to attempt sleep, Cromwell said, "It is not my design for drink or to sleep, but my design is to make what haste I can to be gone." He was gone the next day.

X

Charles II of England was a good-natured king and, at the end, an uncommonly polite one. On February 2, 1685, Charles fell victim to an apoplectic-type seizure while he was having his morning shave. Although his illness (today thought to be a form of Bright's disease) was terminal, Charles's demise was certainly hastened along by his doctors, who determinedly bled him, administered strong emetics, purgatives and clysters, and blistered the poor king's freshly shorn head. Thursday, February 5, found Charles lying in bed surrounded by family, friends, servants and his court. He apologized for the delay—"I have been a most unconscionable time dying, but I hope that you will excuse it." After being bled of sixteen ounces of blood the following morning, Charles made his last recorded request: "Open the curtains that I may once more see day." At 8:30 he lost his speech. By noon he was dead.

X

Henry Fox, the first Baron Holland, was one of the most hated politicians of his day. His great unpopularity persisted into retirement and, in fact, continued to grow, so that by the time of his death (July 1, 1774) he was nearly friendless. His last years were spent in great bitterness and pain, eased only by the deep love he and his wife shared, and his affections for and delight with his sons (whose extravagant lifestyles he willingly subsidized).

One of Fox's only remaining friends was the politician and wit George Selwyn. Selwyn is also remembered for his fascination with corpses and his attendant interest in viewing executions and autopsies. Fox's last recorded moments concern this morbid penchant of Selwyn's. Selwyn called on Fox, then lying on his deathbed at Holland House, and left his card. Fox, after receiving Selwyn's card, said, "If Mr. Selwyn calls again show him up: if I am alive I shall be delighted to see him; and if I am dead, he would like to see me."

X

"There have been good and wise kings, but not many; take them one with another, they are an ordinary set, but **George the Fourth** is the worst I have ever known." So wrote Charles Greville in his memoirs about one of the least loved monarchs in British history. Promiscuous, selfish and capricious, George lived a life of indolence that finally killed him in 1830 at the age of sixty-seven.

In his later years George suffered from gout, arteriosclerosis and a general rapid decline of his internal organs. He would not (even after a series of attacks so severe that his face would turn black for lack of air) modify his excessive habits. A typical breakfast for George in the spring of 1830 was "a pidgeon and beefsteak pie of which he ate two pidgeons and three beefsteaks, three parts of a bottle of Mozelle, a glass of dry champagne, two glasses of port (and) a glass of brandy!"

On the night of June 25, 1830, the king slept in his chair, his hand in that of his friend, Sir W. Waller. He woke at 1:45 A.M., had tea and fell asleep once more, this time for about an hour. After calling for his night-chair (portable toilet) at three o'clock and using same, he said, "I do not think all is right. What shall we do next?" Waller answered, "Return as soon as possible to your chair." The king did so and then gripping Waller's hand more tightly, stared fiercely into his eyes and said, "My dear boy, this is death!" He never spoke again; within minutes his reign was at an end.

X

"I am no more able to refrain from gusts of temper and anger than I am able to keep a cigar out of my mouth." The hard-living newspaper publisher **E. W. Scripps,** who variously controlled about thirty daily newspapers, was very fond of cigars. His prodigious intake of cigars, estimated at thirty to forty a day, caused his doctors great dismay. "I quit going to church mainly because I could not smoke there," he joked in his memoirs.

For the last four years of his life he cruised about the world in his yacht, the *Ohio,* unencumbered by the cares of the newspaper business. On the evening of March 12, 1926, Scripps had dinner aboard the yacht, followed by several hours of conversation and cigar smoking. On retiring Scripps mentioned that he didn't feel well. "Too many cigars this evening, I guess." He died within minutes, and was later buried at sea.

Ⅹ

In early March 1881 the pianist **Nicholas Rubinstein** lay terminally ill in his rooms at the Grand Hotel in Paris. His physician, noting the huge tray of food at Rubinstein's side, admonished him. "You must not eat so much." "Great men always eat a lot," retorted Rubinstein. "Beethoven was a huge eater. Do you know what Schopenhauer said to somebody who was shocked to see him devour his dinner? 'I eat a great deal, sir, because I have a great mind.'" Rubinstein, forty-five years old, not only ate but drank a great deal, and existed on very little sleep. Conductor of the Imperial Russian Music Society, director of the Moscow Conservatory, and the man who first brought Tchaikovsky's works to public attention, he was indeed gifted.

The morning of March 23 found Nicholas feeling considerably improved and hungry. He ordered his lunch—"Oysters! Nothing will do me so much good as a dozen oysters. And an ice afterward." Rubinstein ate the oysters voraciously, and immediately upon finishing was struck with searing pains, causing him to vomit. He then fell unconscious, a state he remained in until he died in the arms of his friend Turgenev the following afternoon.

X

Fats Waller and his manager Wallace Kirkeby were on a train out of Chicago bound for Kansas City in December 1943. Waller was a pianist and composer of enormous talent. (The hit musical *Ain't Misbehavin'* is based on his work.) He was also a man of enormous appetites (whether for food, liquor, music or women), and was completely worn out by his indulgences, a series of one-night performing engagements and a recent bout with influenza. Following a rollicking night in the train's club car, Waller slept all night, through the next day, and into the following night. The train was approaching Kansas City, where it would be held over because of a blizzard.

Kirkeby entered their sleeper at 2:00 A.M. and was struck by how cold it was inside the room. "Jesus, it's cold in here," he remarked to Fats, who was still in bed. "Yeah, Hawkins is sure blowing out there tonight," answered Waller (he was referring to his friend, the saxophone player Coleman Hawkins). A shivering Kirkeby then asked, "Are you warm enough?" "You'll be okay when you get into bed," said Waller.

At six o'clock Kirkeby was awakened by Waller's coughing. Getting up, Kirkeby saw Waller "trembling all over. . . . It seemed he was having a bad dream, but I couldn't wake him." A doctor was sent for, but by the time he arrived Fats Waller was dead. Also being held over at the station was a westbound train, one of whose passengers was the legendary Louis Armstrong. After he heard the news of his friend's death he couldn't stop crying, unable to believe that Waller, only thirty-nine years old, was dead.

X

When William Sidney Porter, known and beloved as **"O. Henry,"** chronicler of turn-of-the-century New York (which he dubbed

"Bagdad on the Subway") and her "four million" (inhabitants), registered at the hospital in which he was to die, it was under the alias of Will S. Parker. (Originally he said, "Call me Dennis. My name will be Dennis in the morning.") Thus his desire for anonymity that had caused Porter to be such a furtive and secretive man during his lifetime was carried out to the end, so much so that no one at the hospital had any idea of the identity of their famous patient.

Porter had been found semi-conscious in his rooms, and after having been rushed to the hospital, was found to be suffering from highly advanced cases of cirrhosis of the liver and diabetes (as well as a seriously dilated heart). These afflictions were no doubt complicated by the nine empty whiskey bottles found under his bed, the remnants of his final spree. At midnight, June 4, 1910, a nurse dimmed the lights in his room. Porter asked that she "turn up the lights"—then, jokingly, quoting from a popular song, "I don't want to go home in the dark." Porter died the following morning after asking his doctor to "Send for Mr. Hall" (his editor).

His funeral had a distinctly O. Henry touch: a wedding had been scheduled for the same time in the same church. The wedding guests allowed the funeral to take precedence, yet as the service was being read for O. Henry, one could hear their voices filtering through the church windows, laughing and chattering.

X

On the morning of November 14, 1916, a company of British infantrymen fanned out on the left flank of an attacking line approaching Beaumont Hamel, France. Among the soldiers spread out in the freezing mud this deadly dark and cold morning was the writer H. H. Munro, better known as **"Saki."** Munro had recently been safe behind lines (in a hospital, stricken with malaria), but had been eager to rejoin his troop and take part in the attack on Beaumont Hamel.

After a rendezvous with the troop commander, the men sat back to rest in this No Man's Land, a still sick and haggard Munro choosing a shallow crater, his back resting up against the lip. He shouted, "Put that bloody cigarette out," at someone, his command followed immediately by the sound of a rifle shot. The men scrambled for the trenches, all except Munro. He had been shot through the head.

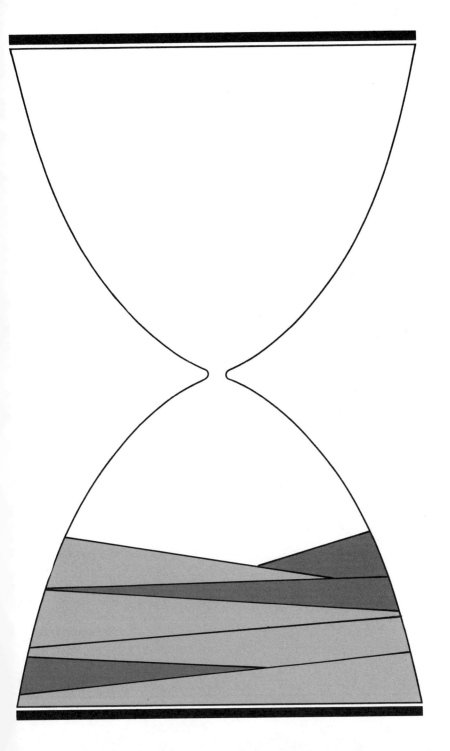

On the morning of April 28, 1881, a Deputy United States Marshal smiled at his prisoner, broke his breech-loading shotgun, and loaded it with two shells, each containing eighteen grains of buckshot. "The man that gets one of these loads will feel it," he said laughing. The prisoner was Billy the Kid, sentenced to hang on May 13, and the marshal was **Robert Olinger,** or "Pecos Bob," as he liked to be called. Tall, well-built, violent, Olinger was picked by Sheriff Pat Garrett specifically because of the mutual hatred shared by Olinger and the Kid. Olinger taunted and tormented Billy relentlessly during the weeks he was guarding him.

At noon Olinger went to lunch and was replaced by Deputy Sheriff Bell. Billy the Kid took up a pistol that had been concealed for him in the outhouse, shot Deputy Bell, picked up the shotgun Olinger had left behind and went over to a window overlooking the yard and street. Hearing the shots, Olinger came running out of the restaurant in which he had been eating lunch, stopping when informed that "the Kid has killed Bell!" Olinger looked up toward the jail, saw the shotgun pointing down from the window and replied, "Yes, and he's killed me too." The Kid fired, and eighteen grains of buckshot ripped through Olinger's chest, killing him instantly.

Ⓧ

An unidentified cowboy once said, "Pat Garrett rustled as many cattle as Billy ever did. Now he's doing Chisum's dirty work." It is true Garrett had rustled cattle; at times the Kid and Garrett had rustled cattle together. A lot of the killing both men did was for cattle barons such as Chisum (sort of Wild West versions of urban gang warfare); a lot of sheriffs and lawmen were under their influence. Like many lawmen before and since, Pat Garrett wasn't above working both sides of the fence.

At this time, however, Garrett was the sheriff of Lincoln County, New Mexico, and **Billy the Kid** had just murdered two of his men, escaping to Pete Maxwell's ranch in the town of Fort Sumner. Midnight, July 14, 1881, found Garrett and his deputies John Poe and Thomas McKinney circling toward a sleeping Maxwell's ranch house. Garrett went inside, woke Maxwell and began questioning him as to the Kid's whereabouts. McKinney and Poe waited quietly in the shadows outside. In the meantime Billy the Kid, after a romantic rendezvous with his girlfriend, was quickly walking, barefoot, toward the Maxwell house. He had a knife in his hand to use for carving himself some beef from a side hanging on Maxwell's porch.

The deputies saw him approaching, but thought he probably was a friend of Maxwell, or Maxwell himself (neither knew the Kid by sight). Reaching the porch, Billy almost fell over the deputies. Instinctively, he drew his .41 caliber revolver and asked, "¿Quién es? ¿Quién es?" McKinney, too startled by the sight of a gun to answer, stood up quickly, caught his spur in a floor board and tripped.

Billy, who had thought the two men were Mexican loafers, became alarmed when he noticed McKinney's sidearms (Mexicans rarely wore them). Backing into Maxwell's pitch-black bedroom, his pistol still trained on the two men in the shadows, he asked Maxwell, "Pete, who are those fellows outside?" At that point he noticed a person sitting beside Maxwell's bed. Billy touched the end of the bed with his left hand, again asking, "Pete,¿quièn es?" Garrett then moved for his pistol. The Kid, confused, not wanting to shoot his friend, leapt backwards, frantically whispering, "¿Quién es? ¿Quién es?"

He never received an answer. Garrett shot twice, one bullet slamming into Billy's chest, the other harmlessly into the wall. Garrett ran outside and excitedly told Poe, "That was the Kid in there, and I think I got him!" "Pat, the Kid wouldn't come to this place," answered Poe. "You shot the wrong man." Garrett considered this briefly. Shaking his head, he said, "I'm sure it was him; I know his voice too well to be mistaken." After a brief conference, the men cautiously approached the room. Maxwell gingerly held a candle to the window. It was indeed Billy the Kid. He was lying on his back, his pistol and knife in either hand, staring at the ceiling. He had been killed almost instantly.

X

On a warm February day in 1908, a two-horse buggy carrying two men bounced down a dirt road in New Mexico. One of the men was the six-foot-five **Pat Garrett,** former lawman, now a cattle rancher. He and his companion, Carl Adamson, were en route to the closing of a business deal that involved the selling of Garrett's ranch, when they overtook Wayne Brazel on the road. Problems with Brazel were delaying the sale, causing bad blood between the two men, above and beyond that of the natural enmity existing between goat and cattle men.

The two parties rode along in virtual silence, which was occasionally broken by a sarcasm, an argumentative remark or a heated exchange. Adamson stopped to relieve himself and while doing so heard Brazel and Garrett arguing. In effect Garrett told Brazel that, one way or another, he would drive Brazel off his land. Then, carrying a Burgess folding shotgun with the right hand, Garrett walked behind the buggy, removed his left glove, undid his pants, and proceeded to urinate. A moment later a .45 caliber bullet hit Garrett in the back of the head, followed by another in his back.

X

In 215 B.C. Roman soldiers, under the direction of the brilliant General Marcellus, attacked the city-state of Syracuse by land and sea. Minutes after the attack began, what seemed like the fury of the gods was loosed on the assaulting troops. The air was filled with masses of stones and darts, killing many of the infantrymen and forcing the rest to flee. From inside the walls stretched long wooden poles attached to cranes that literally grabbed the attacking ships, lifted them high into the air and tossed them back into the sea. Marcellus wisely called for a retreat. The general was more pragmatic than many of his troop, and realized that this extraordinary defense was not the work of the gods but rather **Archimedes,** the seventy-two-year-old mechanical and mathematical giant, and citizen of Syracuse.

The Romans, under Marcellus's orders, waited; the citizens of Syracuse became complacent. In 212 B.C., while a feast went on inside the city, Romans sneaked over the walls and in the morning took over the hungover city. Marcellus had given strict orders that the life of Archimedes be spared and that he was to be sent before the general. While Syracuse was plundered around him Archimedes, oblivious, was intent on a diagram he had drawn in the sand. A Roman soldier entered the house and demanded Archimedes follow him immediately. Archimedes refused to go and said, "Don't step on my circle, you're spoiling it." The soldier stabbed Archimedes, killing him. General Marcellus, on hearing the news, had the soldier executed as a common murderer.

$$\text{Ⅹ}$$

Caecina Paetus, Stoic, was convicted in Rome of conspiracy against Emperor Claudius in A.D. 42. His penalty was to die by his own hand. His wife, **Arria Paetus,** after attempting, and failing, to save him, noticed his courage departing at the moment when he was to kill himself. She then plunged the dagger into her own heart and handed it to her husband saying, "See, it doesn't hurt."

$$\text{Ⅹ}$$

On the fourth of July, 1948, **Georges Bernanos,** French political writer, radical Christian and author of many novels, including *Diary of a Country Priest,* told his wife from his hospital bed that he was dying. A little later he cried out, "Mother, mother," to which the nurse inexplicably replied, "Just wait a moment and I'll go out and look for her in the hall." "You certainly won't find her there," said Bernanos, "because she's dead." The nurse said, "You'll find her in heaven." Bernanos replied, "Certainly I shall find her in heaven." That night he fell into a coma. At 5:00 the following morning he awoke and spoke the names of his children and his wife. He repeated his wife's name three times and died.

X

Marquis **B. Stanislas Jean de Boufflers** was one of the more colorful persons in a colorful age, eighteenth-century France. He was a soldier, explorer, poet and libertine. His love affair with the Comtesse de Sabran was a classic *grande passion*. Boufflers died in 1815 at the age of seventy-seven in the arms of the woman he loved. To her and others around him he said, just before dying, "My friends, believe that I sleep."

X

In 1817 **Germaine de Staël** wrote to a friend, "Every night I suffer from my mother's illness [insomnia], and this lack of sleep makes life too long; there is not enough in it to hold one's interest for twenty-four hours." Her life was not to last much longer. The celebrated author and radical was, as were several of her contemporaries and friends (who included Byron, Napoleon, Talleyrand and Goethe), a living symbol of the Romantic age and spirit.

Although confined to bed for the last ninety days of her life, she nonetheless never stopped entertaining, throwing dinner parties after which the guests would gather around her bedside and listen as the brilliant invalid spoke on a multitude of subjects. "It is truly punishment from heaven," she wrote, "when the world's most active person finds herself so to speak, petrified. . . . But I am not petrified either in mind or heart."

Madame de Staël was horrified at the prospect of either outliving her husband (who was also quite ill) or of dying in her sleep, fears which prompted her to refuse both sleep and opium for a time. On July 12, 1817, she saw and talked politics with Mathieu and the Duke of Orleans. At bedtime that evening de Staël asked for some opium, and was refused. She was to make the same request frequently over the next few hours. Finally her attendant and friend, Fanny Randall, administered what has been recorded as being a rather strong dose. "Now are you going to sleep?" she asked de Staël. "Yes, heavily, like a big peasant woman," answered de Staël. She fell asleep holding Fanny's hand, and never awoke.

X

On September 17, 1921, the explorer **Ernest Shackleton** left London aboard the *Quest,* bound for Antarctica. At 2:00 A.M. on January 5, 1922, the *Quest* lay anchored on Grituiken Harbor. Shackleton whistled for the man keeping watch, Dr. Alexander Macklin, saying upon his arrival, "I can't sleep tonight, can you get me a sleeping draught?" Macklin remarked that Shackleton was covered by only one blanket on this particularly cold night. "Never mind tonight, I can stand the cold." Macklin nevertheless fetched a second blanket for him.

Upon his return they chatted for a while. Macklin ventured to suggest that Shackleton ought to take better care of himself, perhaps slow down a bit. "You are always wanting me to give up something," Shackleton snapped. "What do you want me to give up now?" Macklin was never to answer Shackleton, who died almost immediately after asking this last question.

X

Henry Stanley, the man who found Dr. Livingstone in Africa, was also a reporter, journalist, a soldier in the Confederate army and a soldier in the Union army (both of which he deserted). He died of pleurisy in May 1904. On his deathbed in London, Stanley's mind wandered back to Africa; he said repeatedly, "I want to go into the woods to be free. . . . I want to go home." On the morning of May 10, nearby Big Ben struck the hour and Stanley spoke his last words: "How strange. So that is Time."

X

One of England's greatest men of letters, **Thomas Carlyle,** lasted three weeks longer than the doctors had calculated. During those weeks he could barely speak and dozed much of the time, though in his waking moments his mind remained alert and active. At one point in his last week, the eighty-five-year-old Carlyle began moaning and his niece at his bedside started to cry. He opened his eyes and said to her, "I am not feeling any pain."

On Thursday, February 2, 1881, Carlyle fell into a profound sleep from which he woke only once, when his niece heard him say to himself, "So this is Death—well. . . ." He died the next morning, still sleeping.

X

The illness that killed **Jane Austen** on the morning of July 18, 1817, was not diagnosed correctly until July 18, 1964, when, in the *British Medical Journal* Zachary Cope identified her symptoms as those of Addison's disease. This mysterious illness lasted for three months during which time Austen became totally incapacitated and suffered terribly from back pains. She spent her last days with her sister Cassandra. At six o'clock on the eve of July 17 she suffered an attack of faintness soon followed by torturous pains all over her body. Her sister asked if there was anything she wanted. "Nothing," she answered, "but death."

X

On the afternoon of January 13, 1819, John Taylor began maintaining a vigil at the bedside of his old friend, the poet and satirist **John Wolcot,** who wrote under the pen name of Peter Pindar. Wolcot finally awoke at 10:00 P.M. Taylor leaned over him, told him the hour, and said he had to be leaving shortly. "Is there anything I can do for you?" he asked. "Bring me back my youth," answered Wolcot. He never spoke again, dying peacefully in his sleep the following morning.

X

Historian **William Prescott** wrote to a friend in the winter of 1858–59, "Life is so stale when one has been looking at it for over sixty winters." But to Henry Wadsworth Longfellow who bumped into Prescott in December, the historian seemed cheerful and fresh. He said to Longfellow at this meeting, after chatting for a while, "I am going to shave off my whiskers. They are going gray." Longfellow replied, "Gray hair is becoming." "Becoming," said Prescott, "what do we care about becoming who soon must be going."

Soon afterward Prescott, commenting on a friend's death, said, "The evening of life is coming over those of our generation, and we must be prepared to say farewell to one another." Three days later, on January 27, 1859, Prescott suffered an apoplectic stroke that killed him.

X

After a visit from his sixty-nine-year-old friend **Thomas Bailey Aldrich,** Mark Twain wrote, "Aldrich was here half an hour ago like a breeze from over the fields, with the fragrance still upon his spirit. I am tired waiting for that man to grow old." Aldrich, poet, storywriter and man of letters, *was* astonishingly youthful looking and acting in his later years.

On January 31, 1907, however, Aldrich was suddenly and unexpectedly stricken seriously ill. He was operated on almost immediately (and unsuccessfully) after which he lingered for six weeks. To a visitor Aldrich said, "I myself regard death merely as the passing shadow on a flower." He was taken to his home, at his own request, on March 12. Two days later he died calmly and fully conscious. His last words were spoken to his wife at his side: "In spite of it all, I am going to sleep; put out the lights."

X

The poet **Ebenezer Elliott,** known as the "Corn-Law Rhymer," was seriously ill and confined to his bed on November 17, 1849. On this day he was to enjoy one of his last and most cherished wishes, one that would "smooth my passage to the grave" (as he wrote his future son-in-law and biographer, John Watkins)—his daughter's marriage. Too ill to attend the ceremony, Elliott was content to watch from his window as the couple left for church.

After the wedding his decline was rapid. Eager to remain with his family, he asked if he might live in London with the newlyweds. At one point he said to Watkins, "You see a strange sight, sir; an old man unwilling to die."

Toward the end Elliott was mostly insensible, his thoughts seeming to run to nature and his beloved long walks of old. He often talked in his sleep and dreamed out loud. "I thought I was on the Common, and a child knocked me down with a flower," was one such utterance. "What a strange head your sister has; like a flower, top-heavy!" was another. A short poem (dictated) about a robin who had been nesting by his window was his last coherent act, and his last creation. Elliott died peacefully on December 1.

X

The newspaperman **Thurlow Weed,** although lame and nearly blind, enjoyed a peaceful old age. For one thing, he rarely lacked company. His pet white dove perched on his shoulder, he would receive frequent callers or listen as his daughter Emily read to him. (After one reading he exclaimed, "This is the fiftieth time I've read *David Copperfield.*")

In the fall of 1882 Weed caught a cold and afterward was never really well. Confined to bed, blind, mostly comatose, the old man's world was one of shadows. One night that same year he imagined he was discussing the Civil War with his friends Abraham Lincoln and Winfield Scott. When he was through with this conversation he ordered a carriage, paused, then said, "I want to go home." Weed never spoke again, dying shortly thereafter.

X

Ebenezer Rockwood Hoar served as Attorney-General under Ulysses S. Grant. He was a man known for his wit, common sense and adherence to the law. Hoar died in 1895 at the age of seventy-eight in Boston City Hospital. To a visitor he remarked, not long before his exit from this world, "I am engaged in the not disreputable, but far from attractive, business of dying, and I have one quality especially suitable for it—I have plenty of leisure to attend to it."

X

In 1847 **Joseph John Gurney,** British banker, Quaker and reformer, was thrown from his horse while riding to his home. He was to die a week later. On his last day Gurney fell into a deep sleep from which he awoke for only a moment. He turned to his wife in that moment, and said, "I think I feel a little joyful, dearest."

X

Maud Gonne MacBride, great beauty, lover of the poet Yeats and English supporter of the cause of Irish independence, lived to the age of eighty-seven. The passionate and committed champion of the rights of women and children fell into a coma and died in 1953. Among her last words before gliding into unconsciousness were, "I feel an ineffable joy."

X

Toward the end of her life the suffragist **Lucy Stone** was asked why she did not take a trip to Switzerland to visit the mountains she had always wanted to see. "Oh, why don't I do so many things! It is too late. I shall never do it now. But I have done what I wanted to do. I have helped the women." She had. Lucy Stone literally devoted her life to the nineteenth-century women's movement.

The daughter of a man who believed men had a divine right to lord over women, Stone sent herself through college, almost unheard of in those days. At the time of her marriage in 1855, besides dropping the word "obey" from her wedding vows, Stone and her husband drew up a joint protest against the legal disabilities of women, which was read before the ceremony. The tract drew worldwide attention. She also retained her maiden name, giving birth to the expression, "a Lucy Stoner," to describe any woman making this decision.

Her last editorial (in the *Woman's Journal,* of which she was co-editor with her husband) ended by asking the Boston *Herald* to "use great influence to help men and women go side by side to the ballot box."

Although greatly pleased by suffragette victories in New York, Colorado and New Zealand, Stone would not live to see women get the vote. On October 18, 1893, Lucy Stone was quietly resting at her home in Dorchester, Massachusetts. In the afternoon her daughter Alice saw that Lucy was trying to say something to her. She moved closer. Lucy said, "Make the world better." They were her last words.

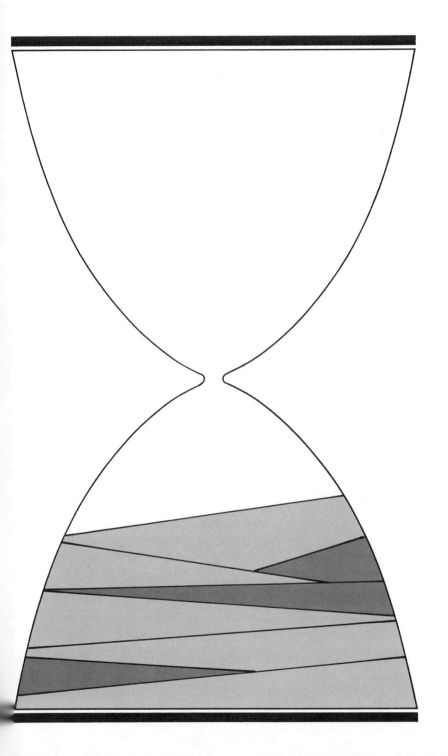

The Roman emperor **Septimius Severus** died in A.D. 211 during an ill-fated expedition to what is now Scotland. He was sixty-six years old, gouty and arthritic and the father of two sons, Antoninus and Geta. Antoninus was continually plotting the murders of both his father and brother, once actually attempting to stab the former in front of thousands of Roman soldiers. Severus has been described as an emperor a cut above the norm for his time, yet one of his last decisions was the initiation of a campaign of genocide against the inhabitants of Scotland, a scheme abandoned after his death.

Severus became very ill during the winter of 211. Shortly before his death he gave his sons some last words of advice: "Do not disagree between yourselves, give money to the soldiers, and despise everyone else." His advice was not heeded; Antoninus had Geta murdered the following year. It is reported that at the moment of death Severus lamented, "I have been all things, and it has profited nothing."

Abd al-Rahman, great military leader of the Arabs, was making inroads in the conquest of Europe when he fought his last battle in A.D. 732 during which he was killed and his armies routed by the Germans. After his death a letter was found with these words of wisdom in it: "I have now reigned above fifty years in victory or peace; beloved by my subjects, dreaded by my enemies and respected by my allies. Riches and honors, power and pleasure have waited on my call. . . . In this situation I have diligently numbered the days of pure and genuine happiness which have fallen to my lot: they amount to FOURTEEN—O, man! place not thy confidence in this present world!"

X

In August 1798 Great Britain won a major naval victory over France known as the Battle of the Nile. Beginning in late afternoon, the battle had continued all through the night, the action hot and apallingly gory. **Captain Aristide Dupetit-Thouars,** the French commander of the eighty-gun ship of the line *Tonnant,* was directing his men when a British cannonball tore off both his legs. Displaying superhuman calm, he refused to go below deck and be attended to by the ship's surgeons.

Instead he had his stumps bandaged, and his men set him in a barrel full of bran. Perched in the barrel, slowly bleeding to death, Dupetit-Thouars proceeded to take charge again, screaming orders and conversing with his officers as the awful fighting raged. His loss of blood steadily weakened him. Turning to a lieutenant he said, "I might lose my head with my blood and do something foolish if I keep the command. It is time I gave it up." His successor chosen, Captain Dupetit-Thouars turned, picked up his pistol, put it to his head and pulled the trigger.

X

On June 12, 1844, the Cuban poet **Plácido** (Gabriel de la Concepción Valdés) was condemned to death for the crime of "high treason." Plácido and ten other men were accused of conspiring to liberate the slave population of Cuba, at that time under Spanish rule. As the eleven men stood before the firing squad Plácido said, "Goodbye O world; here there is no pity for me. Soldiers, fire!" They did, killing the other ten men, but only wounding Plácido. He rose up, pointed to his heart and shouted through the smoke at his executioners, "Will no one have pity upon me? Here, fire here!"

Two bullets then passed through Plácido's heart, killing him instantly.

̆X̆

John Brown, militant abolitionist and freer of slaves, was hanged on December 2, 1859, for leading the raid that sought to liberate Harpers Ferry, Virginia. After reaching the top of the scaffold a cone-shaped black cap was put over Brown's head and he was led to the drop. There he said, "I hope you will not keep me waiting any longer than necessary." A ten-minute delay followed. Finally Brown said, "Be quick," and the order was given.

̆X̆

On a hot August afternoon in 1876 James Butler **"Wild Bill" Hickock** walked into his friend Harry Young's "Number Ten" saloon in Deadwood, South Dakota. The well-dressed Hickock—he was always a bit of a dandy—was invited to join a poker game in progress, which he did, asking only that he be allowed to sit with his back to the wall. It was a request he always made, and one that had always been granted. Hickock was particularly jumpy these days; he had been troubled lately by premonitions of his death, especially since entering Deadwood, where he had been offered the job of marshal. The powers behind the thriving rackets had no desire for Hickock to accept the job, well aware of his past successes in cleaning up other lawless communities.

Hickock wrote to his wife on the day before his death, "Agnes Darling, if such should be we never meet again, while firing my last shot, I will gently breathe the name of my wife—Agnes—and with wishes even for my enemies I will make the plunge and try to swim to the other shore" (the latter sentence was a poetic sentiment in vogue at the time).

108

Hickock therefore was understandably chagrined when the man occupying the wall seat laughed and told him no one was going to attack him. Hickock sat down, but repeatedly made requests that he be allowed to switch seats. He was nervous. This was the first time in his life his back was exposed in such circumstances. As the card game progressed, Hickock began losing to Captain Massie (the man sitting directly in front of him) and asked Harry Young for fifteen dollars worth of checks. As this transaction was taking place, a short, drunken drifter by the name of Jack McCall was drinking cheap whiskey at the bar. He silently eased down the bar until he was standing behind Wild Bill. Hickock was arguing with Captain Massie, complaining to Harry Young, "The old duffer—he broke me on the last hand." McCall leveled his pistol at Hickock's head and fired, shouting, "Take that." Hickock lurched forward, hovered, then crashed backward onto the floor, dead. Even though the bullet had passed through Hickock's brain and into Massie's arm, for moments no one was sure just what had happened. McCall was later convicted of murder and hanged.

The poker hand that lay scattered about Hickock's body (his hands still clutched at imaginary cards) was Aces up Eights: the ace of spades, the ace of clubs, the eight of spades, the eight of clubs, and the jack of diamonds (some say the queen). It is known as the Dead Man's Hand.

X

Major General **George Meade** was one of the most distinguished of those who fought for the Union forces during the American Civil War. He led the Army of the Potomac to victory during the battle of Gettysburg, one of the most horrible conflicts of the war. Meade died of pneumonia, complicated by an old war injury, in 1872. His last reported words were, "I am about crossing a beautiful wide river, and the opposite shore is coming nearer and nearer."

X

On the night of May 2, 1863, the Confederate General **Thomas J. (Stonewall) Jackson** was accidentally shot by his own troops in the confusion of the battle of Chancellorsville. Jackson, a superb tactician, had earned the sobriquet "Stonewall" for his victorious holding actions during the battles of the First Bull Run and Antietam (Sharpsburg). Many feel that Jackson's death proved to be the turning point for the Confederacy.

As a result of his wounds, Jackson's left arm was amputated on May 3. Four days later he contracted pneumonia. On Sunday, May 10, Jackson whispered his last words, "Let us cross the river and rest under the shade of the trees."

X

Jay Cooke was a brilliant entrepreneur who literally kept the United States solvent during the Civil War years by selling bonds and extending credit to the government. On Thursday, February 16, 1905, the Reverend Thomas Cole came to the ailing financier's bedside and recited a "Prayer for the Dying" after which Cooke said, "Amen," adding perceptively, "That was the right prayer." He died a moment later.

X

Joan Crawford, screen star and somewhat less than beloved mother, spent her last years alone in her apartment watching soap operas and old movies on television. Not a total recluse, Crawford did enjoy visitors occasionally and often telephoned and wrote old friends. She also had the assistance and company of a house-keeper.

Crawford faced illness and death with the same rigidity that characterized so many of her screen heroines. A Christian Scientist, Crawford knew she was ill in 1975 but refused absolutely to consult a doctor. The probable cause of her suffering was cancer of the liver or pancreas, though a diagnosis was never made.

By the spring of 1977 the stoic actress was in intense pain and in April her weight was down to a brittle eighty-five pounds. A friend visited her at this time and urged her to go to a hospital. Crawford's reply was typical: "I'll be damned if I'll let myself end up in a cold hospital room with a tube up my nose and another up my ass."

On the morning of May 10, 1977, Crawford's housekeeper relieved another woman who had spent the night sitting by the dying star's bedside. It was clear to the housekeeper that her mistress was very close to death. She began to pray, at first silently, and then aloud. After a few moments Crawford heard the praying and spoke her last coherent words, "Damn it. . . . Don't you dare ask God to help me." Within minutes she was dead.

X

"Another of his triumphant deceptions was that he managed to convince everybody that he was intermittently uncomfortable, but not in pain," wrote Alistair Cooke about actor **Humphrey Bogart** shortly after Bogart's operation for cancer of the esophagus. Bogart, however, was in great pain, and when he awoke on what was to be the last Sunday morning of his life (January 13, 1957), he said to his physician, Dr. Brandsma, "Doc, last night was the worst night of my life—I don't want to go through that again." Later his wife, actress Lauren Bacall, asked him if he was feeling any better. "It's always better in the daylight," replied Bogart. When Bacall left him to drive their children to Sunday School, Bogart was sitting in bed, shaving. "Goodbye, kid," he said, "Hurry back." When she returned he was in a coma. He died the next morning, fifty-seven years old.

⅂

Before going off to his annual vacation in Arizona in February 1954, **Harry Cohn,** head of Columbia Studios and one of the toughest, most feared and most hated producers in Hollywood, picked himself a plot in a Los Angeles cemetery. The sixty-five-year-old Cohn was suffering from serious heart trouble.

One night during his stay at the Biltmore Hotel in Phoenix in 1958, Cohn received word that his close friend L. K. Sidney had died. Cohn and his wife immediately flew to Los Angeles for the funeral. They visited the late Sidney's son, George, a director, and Cohn asked him, "Did you get L. K. a box?" George Sidney replied, "A casket? Yes, Harry." After a pause Cohn said, "Get me a box," and Sidney replied, "I'll get you a box in about thirty-five years."

After the funeral Harry Cohn and his wife flew back to the Biltmore to continue their vacation. That evening as Cohn hosted a hotel party, he fell ill and was taken to his cottage. The next day George Sidney and Cohn's physician arrived at the Cohn cottage just in time to see the producer carried out on a stretcher. "I don't want to be carried out this way," he said. "I want to sit up." When Sidney tried to put a nitroglycerine capsule under his tongue, Cohn spat it out and said, "Get the box."

In the ambulance, just before he died, Cohn said, "It's no use. It's too tough. It's just too tough."

⅂

On January 21, 1952, the ailing eighty-three-year-old writer **Norman Douglas** penned the following note to a friend:

> . . . *Can't stand this damn nonsense any longer.*
> *Can't even wait for you!*
> *Suffering day and night and a trouble to others.*
> *50 grains of luminal should do the trick.*
> *Please make sure that I am definitely dead, and if*
> *possible make out heart trouble as the cause.* . . .

Douglas apparently postponed his decision to kill himself, because the note was never sent but found among his things after his death two weeks later.

On the night of February 5 Douglas said goodnight to his friends, adding, "God be with you, my dears. You keep the old bugger. I shan't need him." When left alone, Douglas removed some pills from his bag and took them. He was found in a coma the next morning, and died on February 7 at 11:00 P.M.

X

Poet **A. E. Housman**'s favorite activity was walking, a pastime his doctors vainly attempted to restrict in his later years. In 1935 when he was seventy-six he told his brother, by letter, that he was following doctor's orders to the extent of walking only twice the permitted distance. At this time he lived in Trinity College on the second floor; he wrote to a friend, "I still go up my forty-four stairs two at a time, but that is in hopes of dropping dead at the top." Housman was terrified of outliving his own physical competence.

In 1936 on the night before his death Housman lay in a nursing home chatting with his doctor for hours, holding his hand. He said, "You have been a good friend to me. I know you have brought me here so I may not commit suicide, and I know you may not help me to it more than the law allows. But I do ask you not to let me have any more unnecessary suffering than you can help." The doctor told him that his sufferings were at an end and then proceeded to tell "a thoroughly naughty story" which amused Housman, who said, "Yes, that's a good one, and tomorrow I shall be telling it again on the Golden Floor." He died quietly the next morning.

⌚

"I have come to the end of my career, and have nothing now to do but to grow old merrily and to die without pain." **Sydney Smith** was to live for twelve more years, and grow old merrily he did. A beloved Anglican clergyman and writer born in 1791, Smith was unusual among his contemporaries in that almost everyone was agreed upon what an enjoyable companion he was. Even the most serious could not resist his high good humor and fanciful storytelling. Although he left behind no shortage of mots, people seemed to remember him as a person who could always make them laugh; he was the sort of person who just is funny, no matter what he might be saying or doing. For the last five years of his life Smith was in great pain, having to endure both asthma and the gout. He was often denied his great pleasures of eating and drinking, at least in the manner to which he had become accustomed.

"I am now tolerably well," he wrote, "but I am weak and taking all proper care of myself; which care consists in eating nothing that I like and doing nothing that I wish." He called his gout, which was causing him extreme discomfort, "the only enemy that I do not wish to have at my feet." He continued, "When I have the gout, I feel as if I was walking on my eyeballs." He was philosophical about it. "What an admirable provision of Providence is the gout! What prevents human beings from making the body a larder or a cellar but the gout? When I feel a pang, I say, 'I know what this is for. I know what you mean. I understand the hint!' and so I extract a little wisdom from the pain."

Smith seemed determined to remain cheerful when on a strict diet. "Ah Charles," he lamented to Charles Fox. "I wish I were allowed even the wing of a roasted butterfly." Even very near the end, when seriously ill, he remained in high spirits, joking and teasing. To a visitor who asked him how he had slept the evening before, Smith answered, "Oh horrid, horrid, my dear fellow! I dreamt I was chained to a rock and being talked to death by Harriet Martineau and Macaulay." By February 1845 he was often semi-conscious, sometimes calling for his dead son Douglas. When told a poor clergyman to whom Smith had granted a small annuity wished to thank him, Smith groaned. "He must not thank me; I am too weak to bear it."

Smith died on February 22, 1845. His last joke, and the last recorded utterance we have, is as follows: Smith's nurse went to the cupboard to get Smith's medicine, but found half a bottle of ink in its place. She facetiously remarked to Smith that his last dose must have been one of ink. "Then bring me all the blotting paper in the house," said Smith.

$$\text{X}$$

The cartoonist **William Murphy,** creator of the comic book characters "Arnold Peck the Human Wreck," and "Henry Henpeck," among others, began his career as a copywriter for the big advertising firms. Dissatisfied with the artificiality of the advertising life, he began writing and drawing underground comic strips. In 1976, while his work was appearing regularly in various comics and the *National Lampoon,* Murphy came down with a pneumonia serious enough to hospitalize him.

One of the last people to see him alive was friend and fellow cartoonist Ted Richards. During this last visit Richards noticed Murphy's teeth were blood-stained, and recalled him asking for a glass of water. After being told he couldn't have water, because he was about to be put on a respirator, Murphy said, "Oh, God, Ted, you don't know." Later in the evening, after being informed that Murphy probably wouldn't last the night, Richards said to him, "You're going to be all right, Murph. We're all pulling for you. Hang on." "We're all pulling for you . . ." echoed an alarmed Murphy. "What do you mean. . . . Am I going to fucking die?" Richards just stared at him.

He later wrote the following: "The entire time I was there a woman in the next bed was crying out every few moments like a moaning metronome. 'Somebody please hold my hand. Somebody please hold my hand.' As we were leaving, her cry interrupted our last goodbye. Willie suddenly stopped talking, looked around for a moment, then bitched, 'Would somebody PLEASE hold her goddamned hand! Jesus Christ, if I ever get out of here all I'm going to remember is 'Will somebody please hold my hand!' He then turned to me grinning and we both shared the humor for a moment, before saying goodbye for the last time."

☒

In 1899 Oliver Wendell Holmes's brother John lay dying in Cambridge, Massachusetts, his family gathered about his bedside. There was some question as to whether John still lived, which was resolved by a nurse who reached under the bedclothes and felt his feet. "Nobody ever died with their feet warm," she whispered. **John Holmes** looked up suddenly and said, "John Rogers did." These were his last words.

John Rogers had been burned at the stake for the crime of heresy in 1555.

X

The death of the great playwright **Lope de Vega** was a national event in Spain in 1635. As the author of more than 1,800 comedies lay dying, he posed a question to the visitors gathered around him. Lope wanted positive assurance that he was going to die because there was something he had always wanted to say, an admission he feared to survive. Assurances of the certainty of his impending demise were given. Lope's confession was, "All right then, I'll say it. Dante makes me sick."

X

Henry Ward Beecher, the most famous preacher of his day, wielded tremendous influence throughout America. As pastor of Brooklyn's Plymouth Church he regularly drew congregations of up to 3,000 persons weekly. Even an adultery scandal did little to diminish his popularity. On March 5, 1887, Beecher lay in bed. As his physician, Dr. Searle, shook his shoulder in an effort to awaken him, Beecher's wife said, "Father, you must get up and dress. It is afternoon and you will have to go to prayer-meeting. Do you hear me?" "Yes," answered Beecher. "I hear but I don't want to get up. I will not go to prayer-meeting tonight. Tell them—" His sentence was left unfinished.

As Beecher had been violently nauseated the night before, it was decided to let him rest. Dr. Searle returned at seven o'clock and woke Beecher. "Raise your hand," he said to Beecher. "Can you raise your hand?" "I can raise it high enough to hit you," smiled Beecher. But he could not. After looking around the room he clasped his wife's hand, gave it a long squeeze and closed his eyes. He never awoke, dying on March 8.

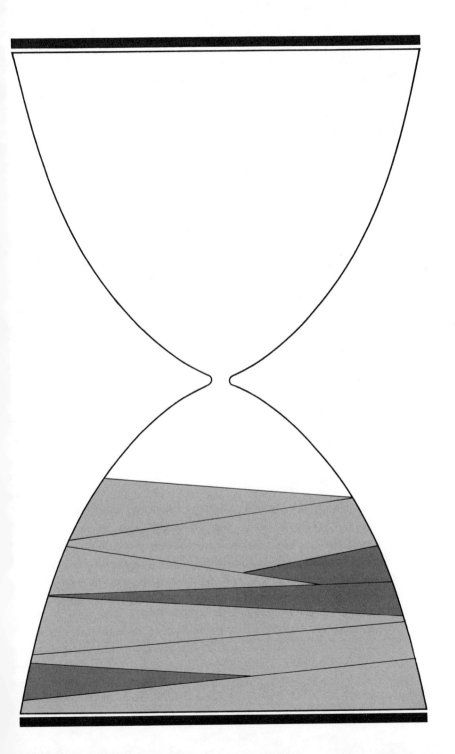

William Henry Jackson, better known as "Zip," was one of the most popular circus side show "freaks" of all time. He was a microcephalic—a person born with a receding forehead and very small skull that tapers to a rounded point—commonly known as a "pinhead." The character and concept of the "pinhead" has become a symbol of sorts in both new wave music and underground comics, used to address the issues of what constitutes intelligence and who the intelligent really are. (Zip Jackson inspired "Zippy the Pinhead," the central character in one of the most brilliant strips being done today, created by Bill Griffith.)

Microcephalics generally have the intelligence of young children, but it is unclear exactly how intelligent or unintelligent Jackson was. He had a highly developed sense of the absurd, was affectionate, friendly and a wonderful showman. He also was under the impression that he owned Barnum's famous traveling museum; Jackson would give Barnum orders and advice, and was known both to hire and dismiss other employees at his own will.

Jackson himself lived a long life, and died financially fairly well off in New York City on April 30, 1926, following a show business career that spanned sixty-seven years. He spent his last days in Bellevue Hospital. It is reported that shortly before his death he turned to his sister and said, "Well, we fooled 'em a long time."

X

The artist and naturalist **John James Audubon** sank in his later years into a senility that saddened his family deeply. He was almost totally divorced from reality and had to be accompanied wherever he went. He spent his last months in silence, responding little to the world around him. Weeks before Audubon's death the family was visited by an old friend, William Bakewell. He spoke to the painter, sitting lost in his mind, and to everyone's great surprise Audubon responded. He looked up at Bakewell and said excitedly, "Yes, yes Billy! You go down that side of Long Pond, and I'll go this side, and we'll get the ducks." They were his final words. He weakened steadily in the days that followed and died on January 27, 1851, at the age of sixty-six.

☒

The enormously prolific writer, **Arnold Bennett,** author of novels, fantasies, self-help manuals and more, died of typhoid in 1931 at the age of sixty-three. He was often delirious in the final weeks. (On one occasion when his wife returned from a concert and said she had been listening to Brahms, Bennett said, "Brahms. Who is Brahms?") In his last lucid moment, Bennett clutched his wife's hand and said, "Everything has gone *wrong,* my dear."

☒

The actor **Maurice Barrymore** was confined to the Long Island Home, a sanitarium at Amityville, for the last four years of his life, stricken with syphilitic insanity. The father of the famous Barrymore triumvirate, once renowned as an actor as well as for his wit, intelligence, dark good looks and athletic ability, was now reduced to an invalid unable to read or write. He was sedated most of the time.

When his children visited he was often rather testy with them. His son Lionel, about to embark on a tour westward, paid a visit shortly before his father's death. "Where did you say you were going?" asked Maurice suspiciously. "West, and then to San Francisco," replied Lionel. "You are a god-damned liar," barked Maurice. "Everyone knows that San Francisco has been destroyed by earthquake and fire." (One year later it was, and John Barrymore was there at the time.) Maurice refused further to acknowledge Lionel's presence.

None of his children was with him when the end came. At 3:55 P.M. on March 26, 1905, Barrymore lay semi-conscious, attended to by a nurse. He opened his eyes, looked at the nurse and smiled. "Our trade falls heavily upon these feeble folk," he said. Five minutes later he died. His last line had been from his unsuccessful play (considered his masterpiece) *Nadjezda*.

⧖

Eugene O'Neill's death was as sad and painful as his life. He spent his last months, the summer and fall of 1953, in Boston in the Hotel Shelton, suffering from a disease that affected the coordination between the nerves and the muscles, causing a gradual but steady deterioration of the bodily functions.

O'Neill's hotel room, which he shared with his wife Carlotta, had a view of Harvard University, the school which he had attended many years before. On a number of occasions the playwright threatened to leap from his window to the Charles River below.

At one point, about two months before his death, O'Neill told his wife, "When I'm dying, don't let a priest or Protestant minister or Salvation Army captain near me. Let me die in dignity. Keep it as simple and brief as possible. No fuss, no man of God there. If there is a God, I'll see him and we'll talk things over."

At the end of November an infection set in and death was very near. Close to the end O'Neill half-sat up in his bed and cried, "I knew it! I knew it! Born in a hotel room and, goddam it, dying in a hotel room!"

He lost consciousness on November 25, 1953, and died, still in a coma, thirty-six hours later on the morning of November 27.

X

Moe Berg played catcher for the Boston Red Sox, spoke twelve languages and was an ingenious and successful spy for the United States during the Second World War. When the ex-baseball player convinced Dr. Antonio Ferri to come to America (after searching for him in a race with the German S.S.), President Roosevelt said, "I see Berg is still catching pretty well."

Berg spent his time after the war reading and studying. In his later years amassing knowledge became almost a compulsion; a familiar sight to patrons of Boston bookstores was Moe Berg surrounded by stacks of volumes, reading. He was very secretive to the end about his war experiences and it wasn't until after his death in 1972 that the public learned something of what he'd accomplished. In May 1972 Moe Berg suffered a fall in his home. He died on May 30 in Clara Maas Hospital in Newark. Just before the end Berg spoke his last words to the nurse at his bedside. They were, "How did the Mets do today?"

X

Eugene Jacques Bullard was the world's first black fighter pilot. He was born in Georgia in 1894 but fled his native town after his father was very nearly lynched. A few years later Bullard went to Europe where he joined the Foreign Legion and distinguished himself as a successful combat aviator in the First World War. Between wars he was a nightclub owner in Paris and friend to the artists and writers of the time (among them Hemingway and Fitzgerald). Bullard spied for the French during World War II and was decorated on numerous occasions.

Bullard worked as an elevator operator in New York City in his later years. In the fall of 1961 he was stricken with stomach cancer. On October 12 Bullard was in Metropolitan Hospital being visited by a friend, Mrs. Louise Fox Connel. He lay in his bed with an oxygen tube in his mouth and down his throat. Suddenly he gasped and his head dropped. Mrs. Connel, believing he was dead, began to cry. Bullard opened his eyes, pulled the tube from his throat and whispered, "Don't fret honey, it's easy." He died a few hours later.

X

A frail, consumptive **Katherine Mansfield** (Kathleen Beauchamp) entered the Gurdjieff Institute, near Fontainebleu, France, on October 16, 1923. She hoped that the Institute's experiment in communal living, where the members strove for a unity of one's intellectual, emotional and physical selves, would help to cure her. Mansfield had lost all faith in traditional medicine and its practitioners, and did not intend to write until she regained her health. She was also convinced she must know herself better ("one must become more in order to write"), a task for which she allotted herself three months.

Her husband, John Middleton Murry, came to the Institute for a week's visit on January 9, 1923. That evening, after resting in the salon below her quarters, Katherine and John rose to go to bed. As they were ascending the staircase, Katherine was overcome by a fit of coughing, inducing a severe hemorrhage.

John later wrote, "Suddenly a great gush of blood poured from her mouth. It seemed to be suffocating her. She gasped out, 'I believe . . . I'm going to die.' " He ran for a doctor, as Katherine, her eyes "wide with terror," sat on her bed, holding her pale hands over her mouth, blood seeping between her fingers. The doctors came instantly, but were unable to do anything for her. She died shortly afterward, at 10:30 P.M.

X

Thomas More spent fifteen months in the Tower of London before he ascended the ladder to the scaffold where he was to be
beheaded in 1535. His charge was treason, because More had
refused to recognize the marriage of Henry VIII and Ann Boleyn.
The ladder was shaky and More said to the lieutenant on duty, "I
pray thee see me safe up, and for my coming down let me shift for
myself."

From the scaffold More asked the people to pray for him and to
remember that he "died the King's good servant, but God's first."
Then the executioner, as was customary, begged his pardon. More
said, "Thou wilt do me this day greater benefit than any mortal
man can be able to give me. Pluck up thy spirit man, and be not
afraid to do thy office. My neck is very short; take heed thy strike
not awry. . . ." Then he blindfolded himself, lay his head face-
down on the block and asked the executioner to wait a minute
while he brushed his beard aside, murmuring that there was no
need for it to suffer as "it had never committed any treason."

X

An aspiring writer visiting **Charles Dickens** in May 1870 asked
him, a trifle tactlessly, in reference to the serialization of *Edwin
Drood,* his latest novel in progress, "But suppose you died before
all the book was written?" "That has occurred to me at times,"
Dickens replied. "One can only work on, you know—work while it is
day."

Dickens did indeed work on. He wrote continually and gave public
readings until the last months of his life, readings that undoubtedly

hastened his demise. These performances were his last great joy in life. He had separated from his wife (far from amicably) a few years earlier, was disappointed and saddened over the apparent unhappiness of his children and disillusioned with the social injustices around him.

Three months after his last reading Dickens was at his country home. He had been suffering from increased paralysis of the left side, but the symptoms were not constant and he could still write and move about, though with difficulty. On June 8, 1870, contrary to his usual habit, he worked all day with only a short lunch break. Shortly before dinner time, sitting across the table from his sister-in-law, Georgina Hogarth, he said suddenly that he must leave for London at once. He rose from his chair and started to topple over. Georgina rushed around the table to hold him up. Dickens was too heavy for her to move to the sofa, so she gently let him sink to the floor. He murmured, "On the ground." Those were his last words; he slipped into a coma and died the next day at the age of fifty-eight.

▛

July 1, 1904, found **Anton Chekhov** amusing his wife, Olga, in their room at the fashionable Hotel Sommer in the German resort town of Badenweiler. Save for a brief walk through the park, Olga had not left his side for three days. She was laughing at the story her husband was telling her and was pleased that he was in such good spirits. Although Chekhov had told a friend in Moscow before his departure that he was "going away to die," his letters home, before June 27, were optimistic about his health, and good-humored: "The only incurable thing about me is my laziness."

In truth, Chekhov was dying from the disease that had plagued him for most of his adult years—tuberculosis. Given his medical training, one can assume he had some notion of the seriousness of his condition, but it appears that he was not aware of how near the end actually was. He wrote to friends that his health was "really on the mend." The constant medical attention, the serenity of his surroundings and his diet of "the same stupid cocoa, the same oatmeal," all conspired to make Chekhov restless. He was making plans to travel to the Italian Lakes when, on June 29, he suffered the first of two heart attacks in two days.

On the morning of July 1 he seemed to be feeling better. After finishing his story to Olga, Chekhov dozed off to awake abruptly at half-past midnight. He asked his wife to send for the doctor, a request she had never heard him make before. While waiting for the doctor to arrive Olga listened to Chekhov, now delirious, rant about a "sailor" and the Japanese. She attempted to ease his sufferings by applying a bag of ice to his heart. Chekhov stopped raving, looked at her sadly and smiled. "Don't put ice on an empty heart," he said.

The doctor arrived and administered an injection of camphor (a stimulant) and suggested to Chekhov that he take some oxygen. Chekhov would have no part of this; he seemed to know he was about to die. "Now nothing is needed. Before they bring it, I'll be a corpse." Champagne was ordered, and a glass offered to Chekhov. He took the glass, smiled at his wife and said, "It is some time since I have drunk champagne." He slowly tipped the glass, drank the champagne, set the glass down and rolled over on his left side. Shortly thereafter he was dead at the age of forty-four.

☒

On a January night in 1905 **Henrik Ibsen** was heard calling in his sleep, "I'm writing! And it's going splendidly!" Ibsen, debilitated by a series of strokes, had in fact already written his last word (the word "Thanks," to his doctor) and it had taken him three days to do so. Attended to by his devoted wife, nurses, a masseur and his family, Ibsen struggled through his last years. He had been unable to walk since 1901, had an increasingly difficult time in speaking and by May 1906 was too weak to stand.

Despite flashes of clarity and strength (his masseur had said concerning Ibsen's condition, "Not too bad. He's sworn a couple of times"), by January 16 he was mostly unconscious. On May 22 he looked up, grasped his doctor's hand and said, "Thank God." Later that afternoon his nurse remarked to others gathered in Ibsen's room that he seemed to be getting a little better. Ibsen spoke up: "On the contrary." It was his last correction, and the last thing he ever said.

X

Arnold Schoenberg began composing at the age of nine; he died at seventy-six still writing music. A musical revolutionary, Schoenberg was the originator of twelve-tone music, an advance which altered the course of modern composition. He died in 1951, his wife and nurse by his side. The last word he spoke was, "Harmony."

BIBLIOGRAPHY

ABBOTT, CHARLES
   Dictionary of National Biography I. London: Oxford University Press,
      1950.
ABD-AL-RAHMAN
   Gibbon, Edward. *The Decline and Fall of the Roman Empire* III. New
      York: Macmillan, 1914.
ADAM, ALEXANDER
   Lockhart, J.G., Esq. *Memoirs of the Life of Sir Walter Scott* I. Paris:
      Baudry's European Library, 1838.
   Scott, Walter. *Familiar Letters* I. Boston: Houghton Mifflin, 1894.
ADAMS, HENRY
   Cater, H.D. *Henry Adams and His Friends.* Boston: Houghton Mifflin,
      1947.
ADAMS, JOHN
   Allison, John M. *Adams and Jefferson: The Story of a Friendship.* Nor-
      man: University of Oklahoma Press, 1966.
   Smith, Page. *John Adams.* Garden City, N.Y.: Doubleday, 1962.
ADAMS, JOHN QUINCY
   Bernis, Samuel. *John Quincy Adams and the Union.* New York: Alfred
      Knopf, 1956.

Hecht, Marie B. *John Quincy Adams: A Personal History of an Independent Man.* New York: Macmillan, 1972.

ADDISON, JOSEPH

Aikin, Lucy. *The Life of Joseph Addison* II. London: Longman, Brown, Green and Longmans, 1843.

Smithers, Peter. *The Life of Joseph Addison.* Oxford: Clarendon Press, 1954.

AGRIPPINA

Abbott, Jacob. *History of Nero.* New York: Harper and Brothers, 1881.

Bishop, John. *Nero: The Man and the Legend.* London: Robert Hale Ltd., 1964.

ALDRICH, THOMAS BAILEY

Greenslet, Ferris. *The Life of Thomas Bailey Aldrich.* Boston and New York: Houghton Mifflin, 1908.

ALLINGHAM, WILLIAM

Allingham, H. and Radford, D., eds. *A Diary.* London: Macmillan, 1907.

ANDRÉ, JOHN

Flexner, James T. *The Traitor and the Spy: Benedict Arnold and John André.* New York: Harcourt, Brace, 1953.

Sargent, W. *The Life and Career of Major John André, Adjutant-General of the British Army in America.* Boston: Tichnor and Fields, 1881.

ARCHIMEDES

Bendick, Jeanne. *Archimedes and the Door of Science.* New York: Franklin Watts, 1962.

ASTOR, JOHN JACOB

Porter, Kenneth W. *John Jacob Astor, Business Man* II. New York: Russell and Russell, 1966.

Smith, A.D.H. *John Jacob Astor: Landlord of New York.* Philadelphia and London: J. B. Lippincott Company, 1929.

AUDUBON, JOHN JAMES

Ford, Alice. *John James Audubon.* Norman: University of Oklahoma Press, 1964.

AUSTEN, JANE

Jenkins, Elizabeth. *Jane Austen.* New York: Pellegrini & Cudahy, 1949.

BANKHEAD, TALLULAH

Brian, Denis. *Tallulah Darling.* New York: Pyramid Books, 1972.

Israel, Lee. *Miss Tallulah Bankhead.* New York: G.P. Putnam's Sons, 1972.

BARNATO, BARNETT (BARNEY)

Lewinsohn, R. *Barney Barnato*. London: George Routledge and Sons Ltd., 1937.

BARRYMORE, ETHEL

Kotsilibas-Davies, James. *Great Times, Good Times: The Odyssey of Maurice Barrymore*. Garden City, N.Y.: Doubleday, 1977.

BARRYMORE, GEORGIANA DREW

Kotsilibas-Davies, James. *Great Times, Good Times: The Odyssey of Maurice Barrymore*. Garden City, N.Y.: Doubleday, 1977.

BARRYMORE, MAURICE

Kotsilibas-Davies, James. *Great Times, Good Times: The Odyssey of Maurice Barrymore*. Garden City, N.Y.: Doubleday, 1977.

BEARD, GEORGE MILLER

"Dr. George Miller Beard," *Dictionary of American Biography*. New York: Charles Scribner's Sons, 1929.

BEECHER, HENRY WARD

Griswold, W.C. *The Life of Henry Ward Beecher*. New York: Hurst and Company, 1888.

Hibben, Paxton. *Henry Ward Beecher: An American Portrait*. New York: The Press of the Readers Club, 1942.

BEERBOHM, JULIUS

Cecil, Lord David. *Max: A Biography*. London: Constable, 1964.

BEETHOVEN, LUDWIG VAN

Schauffler, Robert H. *Beethoven: The Man Who Freed Music*. New York: Doubleday, Doran & Company, 1929.

BENNETT, ARNOLD

Drabble, Margaret. *Arnold Bennett: A Biography*. London: Weidenfeld and Nicolson, 1974.

BERG, MOE

Kaufman, Louis, Fitzgerald, B., and Sewell, T. *Moe Berg: Athlete, Scholar, Spy*. Boston and Toronto: Little, Brown, 1977.

BERNANOS, GEORGES

Speaight, Robert. *Georges Bernanos: A Study of the Man and the Writer*. New York: Liveright, 1974.

BERNHARDT, SARAH

Skinner, Cornelia Otis. *Madame Sarah*. Cambridge: Riverside Press, 1966; Boston: Houghton Mifflin, 1967.

BILLY THE KID (WILLIAM H. BONNEY)

Metz, Leon C. *Pat Garrett: The Story of a Western Lawman*. Norman: University of Oklahoma Press, 1974.

BISMARCK, OTTO VON

Palmer, Alan. *Bismarck.* New York: Charles Scribner's Sons, 1976.

BOGART, HUMPHREY

Bacall, Lauren. *Lauren Bacall By Myself.* New York: Alfred Knopf, 1979.

Hyams, Joe. *Bogart & Bacall: A Love Story.* New York: David McKay, 1975.

BONAPARTE, NAPOLEON

Ludwig, Emil. *Napoleon.* Trans. Eden and Cedar Paul. New York: Modern Library, 1933.

BOUFFLERS, B. STANISLAS JEAN DE, MARQUIS

Webster, Nesta H. *The Chevalier de Boufflers: A Romance of the French Revolution.* London: John Murray, 1925.

BOUHOURS, DOMINIQUE

Andrews, Peter. "Famous Last Apothegms," *Horizon* 19:96 (Jan. 1977).

BRONTË, CHARLOTTE

Gaskell, Mrs. Elizabeth. *The Life of Charlotte Brontë.* New York: E.P. Dutton Everyman's Library, 1960.

Harland, Marion. *Charlotte Brontë at Home.* New York and London: G.P. Putnam's Sons, 1899.

BROOKINGS, ROBERT S.

Hagedorn, Hermann. *Brookings: A Biography.* New York: Macmillan, 1936.

BROWN, JOHN

Nelson, Truman. *The Old Man: John Brown at Harper's Ferry.* New York: Holt, Rinehart and Winston, 1973.

BROWNING, ELIZABETH BARRETT

Irvine, William and Honan, Park. *The Book, the Ring, & the Poet: A Biography of Robert Browning.* New York: McGraw-Hill, 1974.

Taplin, Gardner B. *The Life of Elizabeth Barrett Browning.* New Haven: Yale University Press, 1957.

BULLARD, EUGENE JACQUES

Carisella, P.J. and Ryan, James W. *The Black Swallow of Death: The Incredible Story of Eugene Jacques Bullard, the World's First Black Combat Aviator.* Boston: Marlborough House, 1972.

BURR, AARON

Parmet, Herbert S. and Hecht, Marie B. *Aaron Burr: Portrait of an Ambitious Man.* New York: Macmillan, 1967.

CARLYLE, THOMAS
  Wilson, David A. and MacArthur, David W. *Carlyle in Old Age.* New York: E.P. Dutton, 1934.
CAROLAN, TURLOUGH
  Máille, Tomás Ó., ed. *The Poems of Carolan.* London: The Irish Texts Society, 1916.
CASANOVA, GIACOMO GIROLAMO DE SEINGALT
  Endore, S.G. *Casanova: His Known and Unknown Life.* New York: Blue Ribbon Books, 1932.
CHARLES II
  Ashley, Maurice. *Charles II: The Man and the Statesman.* New York: Praeger, 1977.
  Pearson, Hesketh. *Merry Monarch: The Life and Likeness of Charles II.* New York: Harper & Row, 1960.
CHEKHOV, ANTON
  Hingley, Ronald. *A New Life of Chekhov.* New York: Alfred Knopf, 1976.
  Simmons, Ernest J. *Chekhov: A Biography.* Boston and Toronto: Little, Brown, Atlantic Monthly Press, 1962.
CHOPIN, FRÉDÉRIC
  Weinstock, Herbert. *Chopin: The Man and His Music.* New York: Alfred Knopf, 1949.
  Wierzyński, Kazimierz, *The Life and Death of Chopin.* Trans. Norbert Guterman. New York: Simon and Schuster, 1949.
COHN, HARRY
  Thomas, Bob. *King Cohn: The Life and Times of Harry Cohn.* London: Barne and Rochliffe, 1967.
COMBE, GEORGE
  Gibbon, C. *The Life of George Combe* II. London: Macmillan, 1978.
COOKE, JAY
  Oberholtzer, Ellis P. *Jay Cooke, Financier of the Civil War.* Philadelphia: Jacobs & Company, 1907.
COROT, JEAN
  Schuyler Van Rensselaer, Mrs. (Marianne Griswold). *Six Portraits.* Boston: Houghton Mifflin, 1889.
CRANE, HART
  Unterecker, John. *Voyager: A Life of Hart Crane.* New York: Farrar, Straus and Giroux, 1969.
CRANE, STEPHEN
  Berryman, John. *Stephen Crane.* New York: William Sloane, 1950.

CRAWFORD, JOAN

    Crawford, Christina. *Mommie Dearest.* New York: William Morrow, 1978.

    Thomas, Bob. *Joan Crawford.* New York: Simon and Schuster, 1978.

CROMWELL, OLIVER

    Coruish, F.W. *Life of Oliver Cromwell.* London: M.A. Rivingtons, 1882.

    Hood, Edwin P. *Oliver Cromwell.* London: Hodder and Stoughton, 1882.

DANTON, JACQUES

    Beesley, A.H. *Life of Danton.* London, New York and Bombay: Longmans, Green and Co., 1899.

    Christophe, Robert. *Danton: A Biography.* Trans. Peter Green. London: Arthur Barber Ltd., 1967.

DARWIN, CHARLES

    West, Geoffrey. *Charles Darwin: A Portrait.* New Haven: Yale University Press, 1938.

DICKENS, CHARLES

    Johnson, Edgar. *Charles Dickens: His Tragedy and Triumph.* New York: Simon and Schuster, 1952.

DOSTOEVSKY, FYODOR

    Dostoevsky, Aimée. *Fyodor Dostoevsky: A Study.* New Haven: Yale University Press, 1922.

    Magarshack, David. *Dostoevsky.* London: Seckert and Warburg, 1962.

DOUGLAS, NORMAN

    Holloway, M. *Norman Douglas.* London: Seckert and Warburg, 1976.

DOUGLASS, FREDERICK

    Washington, Booker T. *Frederick Douglass.* Philadelphia and London: G.W. Jacobs, 1907.

DOWSON, ERNEST

    Longaker, Mark. *Ernest Dowson.* Philadelphia: University of Pennsylvania Press; London: Oxford University Press, 1944.

DU BARRY, JEANNE BÉCU, COMTESSE

    Schumacher, K.V. *The Du Barry.* Trans. Dorothy M. Richardson. New York: Harcourt, Brace, 1932.

DUPETIT-THOUARS, ARISTIDE

    Whipple, A.B. and editors of Time-Life Books. *Fighting Sail.* Alexandria, Va.: Time-Life Books, 1978.

EDISON, THOMAS ALVA

    Clark, Ronald W. *Edison: The Man Who Made the Future.* New York: G.P. Putnam's Sons, 1977.

ELIOT, JOHN

   Winslow, Ola E. *John Eliot: Apostle to the Indians.* Boston: Houghton Mifflin, 1968.

ELLIOTT, EBENEZER

   Watkins, J. *Life, Poetry and Letters of Ebenezer Elliott, The Corn-Rhymer.* London, 1850.

FLEGENHEIMER, ARTHUR (DUTCH SCHULTZ)

   Thompson, C. and Raymond, A. *Gang Rule in New York: The Story of a Lawless Era.* New York: Dial Press, 1940.

FOOT, SOLOMON

   Proceedings on the Death of Honorable Solomon Foot. Washington, D.C.: U.S. Government Printing Office, 1866.

FOX, HENRY

   Ilchester, Earl of. *Henry Fox, 1st Lord Holland: His Family and Relations* II. London: John Murray, 1920.

   Riker, T.W. *Henry Fox, 1st Lord Holland: A Study of the Career of an 18th Century Politician* II. Oxford: Clarendon Press, 1911.

FRANKLIN, BENJAMIN

   Block, Seymour S. *Ben Franklin: His Wit, Wisdom and Women.* New York: Hastings House, 1975.

GARRETT, PAT

   Metz, Leon C. *Pat Garrett: The Story of a Western Lawman.* Norman: University of Oklahoma Press, 1974.

GARRISON, WILLIAM LLOYD

   William Lloyd Garrison: The Story of His Life Told by His Children. New York: Century, 1885–89.

GEORGE IV

   Banvard, John. *The Life of George IV, King of England.* New York: Literary and Art Publishing Company, 1880.

   Hibbert, Christopher. *George IV.* London: Alan Lane Ltd., 1973.

   Wellington, Arthur Wellesley, 1st Duke of. *Wellington and His Friends: Letters of the First Duke of Wellington.* Ed. by 7th Duke of Wellington. London: Macmillan; New York: St. Martin's Press, 1965.

GILBERT, WILLIAM SCHWENCK

   Pearson, Hesketh. *Gilbert and Sullivan.* New York: Harper & Row, 1935.

GOETHE, JOHANN WOLFGANG VON

   Lewes, George H. *The Story of Goethe's Life.* Boston: Houghton Mifflin, 1872.

Ludwig, Emil. *Goethe: The History of a Man, 1749–1832.* Trans. Ethel C. Mayne. London and New York: G.P. Putnam's Sons, 1928.

GOLDSMITH, OLIVER

Forster, John. *The Life and Times of Oliver Goldsmith.* London: Bradbury and Evans, 1855.

Gwynn, S. *Oliver Goldsmith.* New York: Henry Holt and Company, 1935.

Wardle, Ralph M. *Oliver Goldsmith.* Lawrence, Kansas: University of Kansas Press, 1957.

GRANVILLE, AUGUSTUS BOZZI

Granville, P. *Autobiography of A.B. Granville, M.D., With a Brief Account of the Last Years of His Life by His Daughter.* London: H.S. King, 1874.

GREEN, JOSEPH HENRY

Green, Joseph Henry. *Spiritual Philosophy* I. Ed. by John Simon. London: Macmillan, 1865.

GURNEY, JOSEPH JOHN

Swift, David E. *Joseph John Gurney: Banker, Reformer and Quaker.* Middletown, Conn.: Wesleyan University Press, 1962.

HARRISON, WILLIAM HENRY

Cleaves, Freeman. *Old Tippecanoe: William Henry Harrison and His Time.* New York and London: Charles Scribner's Sons, 1939.

HEINE, HEINRICH

Browne, Lewis in collaboration with E. Weihl. *That Man Heine.* New York: Macmillan, 1927.

Butler, Eliza. *Heinrich Heine: A Biography.* London: Hogarth Press, 1956.

HENRY IV

Pearson, Heskerth. *Henry of Navarre: The King Who Dared.* New York and Evanston, Ill.: Harper & Row, 1963.

HEWITT, ABRAM

Nevins, Allan. *Abram S. Hewitt.* New York: Harper and Brothers, 1935.

HICKOCK, JAMES BUTLER (WILD BILL)

Rosa, Joseph G. *They Called Him Wild Bill: The Life and Adventures of James Butler Hickock.* Norman: University of Oklahoma Press, 1964.

HOAR, EBENEZER ROCKWOOD

Storey, Moorfield and Emerson, Edward W. *Ebenezer Rockwood Hoar: A Memoir.* Boston and New York: Houghton Mifflin, 1911.

HOBBES, THOMAS
  Laird, John. *Hobbes.* London: Ernest Benn Ltd., 1934.
  Stephen, Leslie. *Hobbes.* London and New York: Macmillan, 1904.
HOLMES, JOHN
  Bowen, Catherine D. *Yankee from Olympus: Justice Holmes and His Family.* Boston: Little, Brown, 1944.
HOPKINS, GERARD MANLEY
  Ruggles, Eleanor. *Gerard Manley Hopkins: A Life.* New York: W.W. Norton, 1944.
HOUSMAN, A.E.
  Housman, Laurence. *A.E. Housman: Some Poems, Some Letters and a Personal Memoir by His Brother.* London: Jonathan Cape, 1937.
HOUSTON, SAMUEL
  James, Marquis. *The Raven: A Biography of Sam Houston.* New York: Blue Ribbon Books, 1929.
HUGO, VICTOR
  Edwards, Samuel. *Victor Hugo: A Tumultuous Life.* New York: David McKay, 1971.
  Richardson, Joanna. *Victor Hugo.* New York: St. Martin's Press, 1976.
HUNTER, WILLIAM
  Mather, G.E. *Two Great Scotsmen: The Brothers William and John Hunter.* Glasgow: James Maclehouse and Sons, 1893.
HUXLEY, ALDOUS
  Huxley, Laura A. *This Timeless Moment: A Personal View of Aldous Huxley.* New York: Farrar, Straus and Giroux, 1968.
IBSEN, HENRIK
  Meyer, Michael. *Ibsen: A Biography.* Garden City, N.Y.: Doubleday, 1971.
JACKSON, THOMAS J. (STONEWALL)
  Lenoir Chambers, *Stonewall Jackson,* vol. 2. New York: William Morrow and Company, 1959.
JACKSON, WILLIAM HENRY (ZIP)
  Drimmer, F. *Very Special People: The Struggles, Loves and Triumphs of Human Oddities* New York: Amjon Publishers, 1973.
JARRY, ALFRED
  Shattuck, Robert. *The Banquet Years: The origins of the avant garde in France, 1885 to World War I.* Revised ed. New York: Vintage Books, 1968.

JEFFERSON, THOMAS

   Allison, John M. *Adams and Jefferson: The Story of a Friendship.* Norman: University of Oklahoma Press, 1966.

   Parton, James. *Life of Thomas Jefferson.* Boston: Houghton Mifflin, 1883.

KEATS, JOHN

   Bate, Walter Jackson. *John Keats.* Cambridge, Mass.: Harvard University Press, 1964.

   Lowell, Amy. *John Keats.* Boston: Houghton Mifflin, 1925.

KIERDORF, FRANK

   Moldea, Dan E. *The Hoffa Wars: Teamsters, Rebels, Politicians, and the Mob.* New York and London: Paddington Press, 1978.

KING, MARTIN LUTHER, JR.

   Lewis, David L. *King: A Critical Biography.* New York: Praeger, 1970.

   Lokos, Lionel. *House Divided: The Life and Legacy of Martin Luther King.* New Rochelle: Arlington House, 1968.

KUSAKABE

   Stevenson, Robert Louis. *Familiar Studies of Men and Books.* New York: Charles Scribner's Sons, 1894.

LABOUCHERE, HENRY

   Labouchere, Algar Thorold. *The Life of Henry Labouchere.* London: Constable, 1913.

LEDBETTER, HUDDIE (LEADBELLY)

   Garvin, Richard M. and Addeo, Edmond G. *The Midnight Special: The Legend of Leadbelly.* New York: Bernard Geis, 1971.

LIGNE, CHARLES JOSEPH, PRINCE DE

   Gilbert, O.P. *The Prince de Ligne: A Gay Marshall of the Old Regime.* Trans. Joseph McCabe. London: Unwin, 1923.

LINDSAY, VACHEL

   Ruggles, Eleanor. *The West-Going Heart: A Life of Vachel Lindsay.* New York: W.W. Norton, 1959.

MACBRIDE, MAUD GONNE

   Cardozo, Nancy. *Lucky Eyes and a High Heart: The Life of Maud Gonne.* Indianapolis and New York: Bobbs-Merrill, 1978.

MAHLER, GUSTAV

   Werfel, Alma in collaboration with E.B. Ashton. *And the Bridge is Love.* New York: Harcourt, Brace, 1958.

MANKIEWICZ, HERMAN

   Meryman, Richard. *Mank: The Wit, World and Life of Herman Mankiewicz.* New York: William Morrow, 1978.

MANSFIELD, KATHERINE

    Berkman, S. *Katherine Mansfield: A Critical Study.* New Haven: Yale University Press; London: Geoffrey Cumberledge, Oxford University Press, 1951.

    Mansfield, Katherine. *Katherine Mansfield's Letters to John Middleton Murry 1913—1922.* London: Constable, 1951.

MARIA THERESA

    Crankshaw, Edward. *Maria Theresa.* New York: Viking Press, 1969.

MARIE ANTOINETTE

    Mayer, Dorothy M. *Marie Antoinette: The Tragic Queen.* New York: Coward McCann, 1968.

MCINTYRE, OSCAR ODD

    Driscoll, Charles B. *The Life of O.O. McIntyre.* New York: Greystone Press, 1938.

MEADE, GEORGE GORDON

    Meade, George. *The Life and Letters of George Gordon Meade, Major-General U.S. Army.* New York: Charles Scribner's Sons, 1913.

METCHNIKOFF, ÉLIE

    Metchnikoff, Olga. *Life of Élie Metchnikoff 1845—1916.* London: Constable, 1921.

MEW, CHARLOTTE

    Mew, Charlotte. *Collected Poems.* Ed. by Alida Monro. London: Gerald Duckworth, 1953.

MEYNELL, ALICE

    Meynell, Viola. *Alice Meynell, A Memoir.* New York: Charles Scribner's Sons, 1929.

MORE, SIR THOMAS

    Paul, L. *Sir Thomas More.* London: Faber & Faber, 1953.

    Sargent, D. *Thomas More.* New York: Sheed and Ward, 1933.

MOREHEAD, JOHN

    Trexler, S. *John A. Morehead.* New York and London: G.P. Putnam's Sons, 1938.

MORRIS, WILLIAM

    Lindsay, J. *William Morris: His Life and Work.* London: Constable, 1975.

MOZART, WOLFGANG AMADEUS

    Davenport, Marcia. *Mozart.* New York: Charles Scribner's Sons, 1932.

    Levey, Michael. *The Life and Death of Mozart.* New York: Stein and Day, 1971.

MUNI, PAUL

    Lawrence, Jerome. *Actor: The Life and Times of Paul Muni.* New York: G.P. Putnam's Sons, 1971.

MUNRO, H.H. (SAKI)

    Gillen, Charles. *H. H. Munro (Saki).* New York: Twayne Publishers, 1969.

MURPHY, WILLIAM

    Arcade: The Comics Revue I:6 (Summer 1976). The Print Mint Inc.

    The Apex Treasury of Underground Comics. Ed. by D. Donahue and S. Goodrick. Apex Novelties, 1974.

    Willie Murphy Flamed Out Funnies 2. Ed. by R. Fletcher. San Francisco: Rip Off Press, 1976.

NERO

    Abbott, Jacob. *History of Nero.* New York: Harper and Brothers, 1881.

    Bishop, John. *Nero: The Man and the Legend.* London: Robert Hale Ltd., 1964.

    Grant, Michael. *Nero.* London: Weidenfeld and Nicolson, 1970.

    Weigall, Arthur. *Nero, The Singing Emperor of Rome.* Garden City: Garden City Publishing Company, 1930.

OLINGER, ROBERT

    Metz, Leon C. *Pat Garrett: The Story of a Western Lawman.* Norman: University of Oklahoma Press, 1974.

O'NEILL, EUGENE

    Sheaffer, Louis. *O'Neill: Son and Artist.* Boston and Toronto: 1973.

PAETUS, ARRIA

    Anthon, Charles. *A Classical Dictionary.* New York: Harper and Brothers, 1847.

PAINE, THOMAS

    Hawke, David F. *Paine.* New York: Harper & Row, 1974.

PARNELL, CHARLES

    Lyons, Francis S.L. *Charles Stewart Parnell.* New York: Oxford University Press, 1977.

PIAF, EDITH

    Berteaut, Simone. *Piaf: A Biography.* New York: Harper & Row, 1969.

PICASSO, PABLO

    "Pablo Picasso." *Time* 101:17 (April 23, 1973).

PICCOLO, BRIAN

    Morris, Jean. *Brian Piccolo: A Short Season.* New York: Dell, 1971.

PIRANDELLO, LUIGI

Giudice, Gaspari. *Pirandello: A Biography.* Trans. Alistair Hamilton. London, Toronto and New York: Oxford University Press, 1975.

PITT, WILLIAM

Stanhope, E. *Life of Pitt.* London: John Murray, 1862.

PLÁCIDO (GABRIEL DE LA CONCEPCIÓN VALDÉS)

Stimson, Frederick. *Cuba's Romantic Poet: The Story of Plácido.* Chapel Hill, N.C.: University of North Carolina Press, 1974.

POE, EDGAR ALLAN

Allen, Hervey. *Israfel: The Life and Times of Edgar Allan Poe.* New York: George H. Doran, 1926; 1934.

Bittner, William. *Poe: A Biography.* Boston: Little, Brown, Atlantic Monthly Press, 1962.

POPE, ALEXANDER

Paston, George (pseudonym for Emily M. Symonds). *Mr. Pope, His Life and Times.* London, Hutchinson and Company, 1909.

PORTER, WILLIAM SYDNEY (O. HENRY)

Current-García, Eugene. *O. Henry (William Syndey Porter.)* New York: Twayne Publishing, 1965.

Davis, Robert H. and Maurice, Arthur B. *The Caliph of Bagdad: Being Arabian Nights Flashes of the Life, Letters and Work of O. Henry.* New York: D. Appleton, 1931.

Langford, Gerald. *Alias O. Henry: A Biography of William Sydney Porter.* New York: Macmillan, 1957.

Smith, C.A. *O. Henry.* Garden City, N.Y.: Page and Company, 1916.

PRESCOTT, WILLIAM

Gardiner, C.H. *William Hickling Prescott: A Biography.* Austin: University of Texas Press, 1969.

RALEIGH, SIR WALTER

Selincourt, H.D. *Great Raleigh.* London: Methuen & Company, 1908.

Thompson, E. *Sir Walter Raleigh: Last of the Elizabethans.* New Haven: Yale University Press, 1936.

RASPUTIN, GRIGORI EFFIMOVICH

Rasputin, Maria and Barham, Patte. *Rasputin: The Man Behind the Myth, A Personal Memoir.* Englewood Cliffs, N.J.: Prentice-Hall, 1977.

Wilson, Colin. *Rasputin and the Fall of the Romanovs.* New York: Farrar, Straus, 1964.

RHODES, CECIL

    Marlowe, J. *Cecil Rhodes: The Anatomy of Empire.* London: Paul Elek Books, 1972.

RODIN, AUGUSTE

    Descharnes, Robert and Chabrun, Jean. *Auguste Rodin.* New York: Viking Press Studio Book, 1967.

RUBINSTEIN, NICHOLAS

    Bowen, Catherine D. *Free Artist: The Story of Anton and Nicholas Rubinstein.* New York: Random House, 1939.

RUNYON, DAMON

    Hoyt, Edwin. *A Gentleman of Broadway.* Boston: Little, Brown, 1964.

RYBAKOFF, JACK

    Le Comte, Edward S., ed. *Dictionary of Last Words.* New York: Philosophical Library, 1955.

SCHOENBERG, ARNOLD

    Reich, Willi. *Schoenberg: A Critical Biography.* Trans. Leo Black. New York: Praeger, 1971.

SCRIPPS, EDWARD WYLLIS

    Cochran, Negley D. *E.W. Scripps.* Westport, Conn.: Greenwood Press, 1972.

    Gardner, Gilson. *Lusty Scripps: The Life of E.W. Scripps.* New York: Vanguard Press, 1932.

    Scripps, E.W. *Damned Old Crank: A Self-Portrait.* Ed. by Charles R. McCabe. New York: Harper & Row, 1951.

SEVERUS, SEPTIMUS

    Birley, Anthony. *Septimus Severus, The African Emperor.* London: Eyre and Spottiswoode, 1971.

SHACKLETON, ERNEST

    Wild, Commander Frank, C.B.E. *Shackleton's Last Voyage: The Story of the Quest in Official Journal and Private Diary kept by Dr. A.H. Macklin.* London, New York, Toronto and Melbourne: Cassell and Co., 1923.

SHAW, GEORGE BERNARD

    Ervine, St. John G. *Bernard Shaw: His Life, Work, and Friends.* London: Constable, 1956.

SMITH, SYDNEY

    Pearson, Hesketh. *The Smith of Smiths: Being the Life, Wit, and Humour of Sydney Smith.* New York and London: Harper and Brothers, 1934.

Russell, G.W.E. *English Men of Letters.* Ed. by J. Morley. New York: Macmillan, 1905.

SOCRATES

Plato. *Phaedo in the Works of Plato.* Trans. by Benjamin Jowett and ed. by I. Edman. New York: Modern Library, 1956.

STAËL, GERMAINE DE

Herold, C. *Mistress to an Age: A Life of Madame de Staël.* Indianapolis and New York: Bobbs-Merrill, 1958.

Andrews, Wayne. *Germaine: The Portrait of Madame de Staël.* New York: Atheneum, 1963.

STANLEY, HENRY

Hall, Richard S. *Stanley: An Adventurer Explored.* Boston: Houghton Mifflin, 1975.

STEVENSON, ROBERT LOUIS

Daiches, David. *Robert Louis Stevenson and His World.* London: Thames and Hudson, 1973.

Furnas, Joseph C. *Voyage to Windward: The Life of Robert Louis Stevenson.* New York: William Sloane, 1951.

Hennessy, J.P. *Robert Louis Stevenson.* New York: Simon and Schuster, 1974.

STONE, LUCY

Blackwell, Alice S. *Lucy Stone: A Pioneer of Woman's Rights.* Boston: Little, Brown, 1930.

Hays (Rice), Elinor. *Morning Star: A Biography of Lucy Stone.* New York: Harcourt, Brace, 1961.

Heath, E.M. *The Story of Lucy Stone: Pioneer.* London: Allenson and Co., 1935.

STRACHEY, LYTTON

Holroyd, Michael. *Lytton Strachey: A Critical Biography.* New York: Holt, Rinehart and Winston, 1968.

THOMAS, DYLAN

Ferris, Paul. *Dylan Thomas: A Biography.* New York: Dial Press, 1977.

THOREAU, HENRY DAVID

Canby, Henry S. *Thoreau.* Boston: Houghton Mifflin, 1939.

Krutch, Joseph Wood. *Henry David Thoreau.* New York: William Sloane, 1948.

Meltzer, Milton and Harding, Walter. *A Thoreau Profile.* New York: Thomas Y. Crowell, 1962.

VAN GOGH, VINCENT

Hanson, Lawrence and Elisabeth. *Passionate Pilgrim: The Life of Vincent Van Gogh.* New York: Random House, 1955.

VEGA, LOPE DE

Andrews, Peter. "Famous Last Apothegms," *Horizon* 19:16 (Jan. 1977).

WALKER, JIMMY

Fowler, G. *Beau James: The Life and Times of Jimmy Walker.* New York: Viking Press, 1949.

WALLER, FATS

Waller, Maurice and Calabrese, Anthony. *Fats Waller.* New York: Schirmer Books, 1977.

WASHINGTON, GEORGE

Irving, Washington. *Life of George Washington.* Port Washington, N.Y.: Sleepy Hollow Restorations, 1978.

WEBSTER, DANIEL

Curtis, George Ticknor. *Life of Daniel Webster.* New York: D. Appleton, 1893.

WEED, THURLOW

Van Deusen, Glyndon G. *Thurlow Weed: Wizard of the Lobby.* Boston: Little, Brown, 1947.

WESLEY, JOHN

Winchester, C.T. *The Life of John Wesley.* New York: Macmillan, 1906.

WILDE, OSCAR

Hyde, H. Montgomery. *Oscar Wilde.* New York: Farrar, Straus and Giroux, 1975.

Pearson, Hesketh. *Oscar Wilde: His Life and Wit.* New York and London: Harper and Brothers, 1946.

WILSON, WOODROW

Hale, William B. *Woodrow Wilson: The Story of His Life.* New York: Doubleday, Page and Company, 1912.

Walworth, Arthur. *Woodrow Wilson,* 2nd rev. ed. Boston: Houghton Mifflin, 1965.

WOLCOT, JOHN

Girtin, Tom. *Doctor with Two Aunts.* Hutchinson & Co., Ltd. of London, 1959.

WOOLF, VIRGINIA

Bell, Quentin. *Virginia Woolf.* New York: Harcourt Brace Jovanovich, 1972.

WYCHERLEY, WILLIAM

Vernon, P.F. *William Wycherley*. London: Longmans, Green and Company for the British Council and the National Book League, 1965.

Wycherley, William. *The Country Wife* and *The Plain Dealer* in *The Belles-Lettres Series*, Section III. Ed. by G.B. Churchill. Boston, New York, Chicago and London: D.C. Heath, 1924.

Wycherley, William. in *The Mermaid Series: The Best Plays of the Old Dramatists*. Ed. by W.C. Ward. London: Viztelly and Co., 1888.

WYLIE, ELINOR

Gray, Thomas A. *Elinor Wylie*. New York: Twayne Publishers, 1969.

Hoyt, N. *Elinor Wylie: The Portrait of an Unknown Lady*. Indianapolis and New York: Bobbs-Merrill, 1935.

ZIEGFELD, FLORENZ

Cantor, Eddie and Freedman, David. *Ziegfeld, The Great Glorifier*. New York: A.H. King, 1934.

Carter, Randolph. *The World of Flo Ziegfeld*. New York: Praeger, 1974.

We have also used numerous biographical dictionaries and encyclopedias as well as standard encyclopedias.